W9-AGC-309

Sparkling Jewels, Pearls of Wisdom

By Edie McGinnis

KANSAS CITY STAR BOOKS

Sparkling Jewels, Pearls of Wisdom

by Edie McGinnis

Edited by Judy Pearlstein
Technical Editor: Peggy Hutinett
Book Design by Vicky Frenkel
Photography by Krissy Krauser
Production assistance by Jo Ann Groves

Published by Kansas City Star Books
1729 Grand Blvd., Kansas City, Missouri 64108

First edition, first printing
ISBN-13: 978-1-933466-03-3
ISBN-10: 1-933466-03-0

Printed in the United States of America by
Walsworth Publishing Co.

To order copies, call StarInfo, (816-234-4636)

www.PickleDish.com

The Quilter's Home Page

About the Author

Edie McGinnis is a *Kansas City Star* author and editor with a unique perspective: she is a member of *The Star's* staff. Since she went to work there in April of 1987, she has been an advocate for the revival of *The Star's* tradition of publishing quilt blocks. She is now part of the Star Books staff.

This is the eighth quilt book Edie has written for *The Kansas City Star*. She writes a column for *The Star's* quilt website, PickleDish.com. *The Star* has also published single patterns of two quilts Edie has designed.

Edie lectures on *The Kansas City Star* quilt patterns, their history and the designers who worked at *The Star* when the patterns were published. She has been quilting for about 30 years and is a member of The American Quilting Society and The Quilters Guild of Greater Kansas City.

Dedication

To the rowdy girls in the sweat shop: Margaret, Rosemary, Peggy, Carol, Brenda, Karlene, Judy L. and Judy H., Clara, Linda, Peggy McF., Sue, and Shari, what in the world would I do without you people!

To my family, Casey and Courtney McGinnis, Michael and Sarah McGinnis, and Joe McGinnis - your mama loves you.

Acknowledgements

I don't know how I would ever get through a book without the people who help me by testing patterns, listening to my crazy ideas, critiquing, laughing with me (maybe it's really at me) and those that go the extra mile by doing not one pattern but two or three.

Many thanks go to my wonderful friends who tested the patterns: Margaret Falen, Grain Valley, Corky and Peggy Hutinett, Raytown, Carol Christopher, Blue Springs, Karlene Cooper of Kansas City, Rosemary Garten, Linda Kriesel, Dee Clevenger, Judy Lovell, Clara Diaz, Judy Hill, and Brenda Butcher, all of Independence, Missouri. Thanks also to the construction crew in Illinois: Shari McMillan, Peggy McFeeters and Sue McNamara. Bless Karlene Cooper of Kansas City, Missouri, for letting us all gather at her home to sew time and time again.

Thanks to the couples you will meet in the following pages for sharing their stories and their wisdom.

Thanks also go to the wonderful people at Quilter's Station in Lee's Summit, Missouri. Rita Briner, owner and friend, has an uncanny eye for choosing fabrics. Not only did she help with the selection of the fabric for *Diamonds Are . . .* and *Amethyst and Emeralds*, among others, she also made the binding for all the quilts, quilted and bound the table runner, and helped whip binding down so the quilts would be ready for the photo shoot. (If you are getting the idea that I was really in a time crunch, you are right.) Karen Kriens made the punch needle project and Mary Andrews and Jane Miller helped sew binding in place.

Thanks to my sister, Stormy Lee van den Houten, of Eugene, Oregon, for lending her lovely handmade bobbin lace for photography and for making the bride's garter. She is an expert lace maker and I am fortunate to have had her to call on for help with this book.

Thanks to my editor, Judy Pearlstein, for coordinating everything and clearing up my sometimes muddled thoughts. Thanks to Krissy Krauser, my photographer, for the lovely pictures and Jo Ann Groves for her imaging skills. Thanks also to Vicky Frenkel for making these pages look so lovely.

Two quilters worked on the quilts in this book. Mary Hibbs of Country Lane Quilting, Lee's Summit, Missouri, quilted the featured quilt, *Diamonds Are . . .* Mary's quilting turned a lovely quilt into a masterpiece. Her website is www.countrylanequilting.com and she can be reached at 816-350-2002. Thank you, Mary.

Nedra Forbes of Nedra Quilts in Liberty, Missouri, quilted the other quilts. She did a fantastic job on all. The pillow tuck and the border on the *Amethysts and Emeralds* have a 1" crosshatch that truly enhances the beauty of the quilt. Thank you, Nedra, for all your long hours and hard work. You may phone Nedra at 816-781-0182 for an appointment.

As always, thanks to Doug Weaver for having so much faith in me. It's a real privilege to work for him.

TABLE OF CONTENTS

INTRODUCTION

Have you ever gone to a wedding reception and seen a couple who has been married for many years dance with one another? They know without a doubt the next step and move their partner will make. I find successful marriages so heartening in this day and age. It inspires hope for all couples who believe in the dream of "happily ever after."

I often sat in the pew behind Richard and Betty Connell in church and I always enjoyed seeing the two together. Since he is quite a bit taller than she, he would have to tilt his head in her direction if she whispered something to him. When Richard and Betty look at each other, you can see the love they have for each other shining in their eyes. Both were blessed with a good sense of humor and are two of the kindest people I have ever met. They have been married for 52 years now in spite of the bumps in the road that every couple meets. They, like other long married couples, figured out a way to resolve their differences and live in love and harmony.

I am really fortunate to know quite a few couples who have been married more than 40 years. You are particularly lucky, too, for you will be able to meet some of my friends who have successful marriages. Not only are these couples happily married, they would choose to spend their lives with the same person if they had it all to do over again. They also offer some pearls of wisdom to people getting married now.

Along with their enchanting stories, are patterns and designs for jewel quilts. They are quilts that sparkle and dazzle. All have some type of jewel in the pattern name. When you put the blocks together, you will find the most amazing secondary patterns emerging. The quilts are an absolute delight to behold. They all have so much movement, so much going on, that you will never tire of looking at them.

Some of the patterns were very difficult to piece whether you were sewing by hand or by machine, so these patterns have been changed to paper pieced patterns. The Star Sapphire block had curves in all the pieces. I changed that to a paper pieced pattern and removed the curves in the process. Even without the curves, the pattern retains the appearance of facets.

I hope you enjoy sifting through these jewels and make a few gems of your own.

BEN AND NORMA PHILLIPS

Meet Ben and Norma Phillips. They have been married for 49 years and have three children and seven grandchildren. Ben and Norma recently built a new house in Parkville, Missouri. When friends asked them why they were building a new home when many of their friends were downsizing, the reply was, "Well, if not now, when?"

They met at work. Both worked for Procter & Gamble in Kansas City, Kansas. Norma was hired as a secretary in the cost department after being recommended by her high school guidance counselor because of her exceptional typing skills. At the time, Ben was already employed in the cost department as an accountant where he was biding his time until a position opened in the electrical department. He was in the process of getting an engineering degree from Finley Engineering College.

Ben asked Norma out. Their first date was to a Wyandotte High School football game. Both had graduated from high school there and both enjoyed going to see the games at their alma mater. They dated for 10 months before they married in a small formal ceremony with one attendant each.

Norma thought Ben was the man for her because they had the same values and goals. Not to mention the fact that she enjoyed his company. Ben said, "I always felt good when I was with her." The same qualities that drew them together have remained constant throughout the years.

When asked if she would do it over again, Norma answered, "Oh yes. We have had a wonderful life with bountiful blessings. Our children are our best friends and have gifted us with seven grandchildren." Ben's reply was short and sweet. "Yes."

The two have enjoyed traveling. They used to take the children camping at every opportunity. They camped all over Mexico.

One time, Ben called the consulate to make sure everything was safe for their trip. The man he spoke to told him he thought it would be wise if the campers had a gun because of the bandits roaming around. Ben didn't follow that particular piece of advice. He had more than just a little trouble visualizing himself standing at the tent flap with a gun in his hand.

Ben and Norma say they are still together after all these years because they still love each other and because they always worked together for the best interest of their family instead of themselves. They had goals and they stuck to their plan.

When asked if they had any advice for couples getting married today, Norma offered this piece of wisdom, "Communicate. Forget petty differences and concentrate on doing things that both of you enjoy. Spend time together and don't worry so much if someone else has more 'things' than you do. Put your spouse first. Enjoy each day and give thanks always for blessings." Ben followed with this advice, "Remember that your marriage is a partnership and you both must pull together to make it a success."

ROTARY CUTTING INSTRUCTIONS

Much of the time people assume they can't use templates and rotary cut their fabric. That assumption is inaccurate. Here's how you can use templates and your rotary cutter.

1. Cut out a template, including seam allowances, using template plastic.

2. Cut a strip across the width of your fabric to straighten it.

3. Measure the height of the template.

4. Using your rotary cutter, cut a strip equal to the height of the template across the fabric.

5. Place the template on the strip.

6. Butt the ruler up to the template, pull the template away and make the cut with your rotary cutter.

7. Replace the template on the strip. Line up the edge of the template with the cut you just made, butt the ruler up to the template, pull the template away and cut the opposing side of the piece.

8. Continue on in this manner until all your pieces are cut.

The next method is done by cutting the template the finished size.

1. Cut a strip across the width of the fabric that measures the size of the template plus 1/2 inch.

2. Put a piece of double-sided sticky tape on the reverse side of the template. This will hold the template in place.

3. Place the template on the fabric and gently butt an Add-A-Quarter ruler up to the edge of the template and cut, using your rotary cutter.

4. Butt the Add-A-Quarter ruler up against the next edge of the template and cut that side. Continue in this manner until you have cut each side of the desired piece.

5. Move the template and continue cutting until you have gone all the way across the strip of the fabric.

Give this a try. You can really be speedy and cut through multiple layers, if you wish. You can find an Add-A-Quarter ruler at your local quilt shop.

Diamonds Are...

DIAMONDS ARE ...

Designed by Edie McGinnis, quilted by Mary Hibbs of Country Lane Quilting, Lee's Summit, Missouri. This quilt is put together using the test blocks made for the book. Each person who sewed for the quilt is given credit on the pages that follow.

DIAMONDS ARE....

79" x 96"

Fabric Requirements:

- 4 yards light batik for the background, includes framing border
- 5 yards of dark mottled blue batik – includes binding, setting triangles and borders
- 2 yards of teal/navy batik
- 1 yard burgundy batik
- 3/4 yard mottled medium blue batik
- 3/4 yard burgundy/green batik
- 3/4 yard medium blue batik

Follow the instructions for each block. After putting all of the blocks together, follow the placement chart and sew the blocks together in diagonal strips. Do not remove the paper from the paper pieced blocks until you have the entire quilt top sewn together. You will need to cut 14 setting triangles and 4 corner triangles.

To make the setting triangles, cut 4 – 18 1/4" squares from the dark fabric. Cut each square from corner to corner on the diagonal twice. You will have 2 pieces left over.

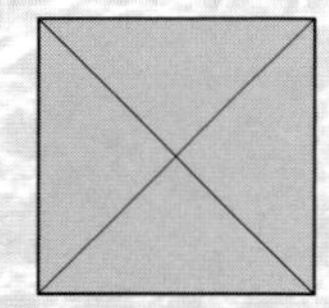

For the corner squares, cut 2 – 9 3/8" squares. Cut each square from corner to corner on the diagonal.

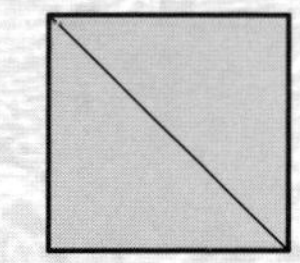

Sew a setting triangle to the top and bottom of each diagonal strip unless the strip starts or ends at a corner. In that case, use one of the corner triangles. You should be able to determine which triangle to use by following the placement diagram.

Sew the strips together. Measure the quilt through the center from top to bottom. Cut 2" border strips from the light fabric. The length will need to equal your measurement. Sew the strips to the sides of the quilt.

Now measure the quilt through the center from side to side. Cut 2" border strips to equal your center measurement. Sew the strips to the top and bottom of the quilt.

Now cut 3 1/2" strips from the dark fabric for the outer borders. Measure the quilt again through the center from top to bottom. Piece together enough strips to equal that measurement. Sew a strip to each side of the quilt.

Measure the quilt through the center from side to side. Piece together enough strips to equal that measurement. Sew one strip to the top and one to the bottom of the quilt.

Layer your quilt with backing and batting and quilt.

Diamond Cluster in a Frame

DIAMOND CLUSTER IN A FRAME

Made by Margaret Falen, Grain Valley, Missouri.

DIAMOND CLUSTER IN A FRAME

12" block

You will need to make four of these blocks for the quilt.

For EACH block, cut:

- 4 diamonds using template Dr from the dark fabric

- 4 diamonds using template D from the medium light fabric and 4 – 2 1/2" x 8 1/2" rectangles from the same fabric (template B)

- 1 - 5 1/4" square from the background fabric (template C). Cut the square from corner to corner on both diagonals making quarter square triangles.

- 4 – 2 1/2" squares of background fabric (template A)

- 4 – 2 1/2" squares of medium fabric (template A)

Begin by piecing the center section of the block. Sew a dark Dr diamond to the left side of a C triangle. Add a medium light D diamond to the right side of the triangle. As soon as you hit the seam line, stop and take a couple of back stitches. DO NOT SEW INTO THE SEAM LINE. If you are not sure where to stop sewing, mark all your pieces with a dot where the seam lines intersect. Punch a hole in each corner of your template with a 1/8" punch, then mark a dot in each corner of each piece. Align the dots, then sew. Make 4 of these units.

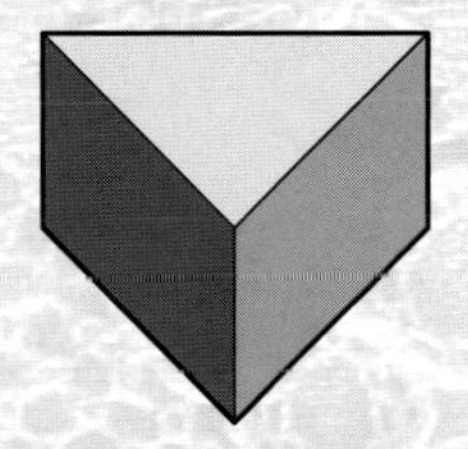

Now add an A square to each of the units. Do not sew into the seam line. They should now look like this.

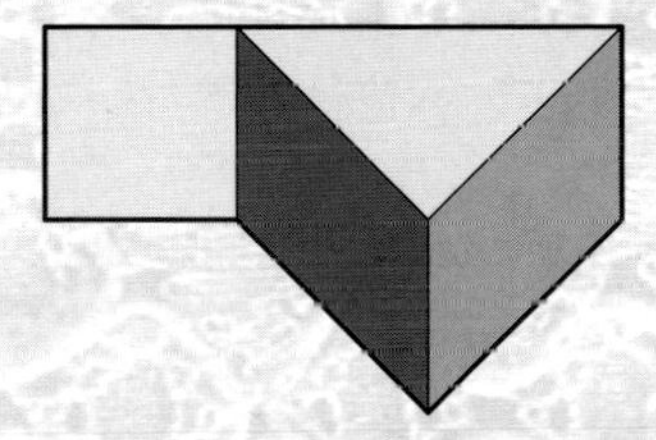

To join the units, sew two pairs of diamonds that have the squares attached to make half of the star. Do this twice, then sew the two together. Set your sewing machine on the longest stitch. Baste a couple of stitches at the beginning of the seam. Raise your presser foot and move to the first part of the star that meets and add a couple of basting stitches at that point. Then move onto the center and baste a few stitches. Go on to the last point where the star meets and baste again and finally baste at the end of the seam line. Open up the block.

Check to make sure all your points match. Reset your machine and sew the seams together if you're happy with the points.

Now sew an A square to each end of a B rectangle. Make two of these strips.

Sew a B rectangle to opposing sides of the center star.

Add the strips with the squares on the ends to the top and bottom of the star to complete the block.

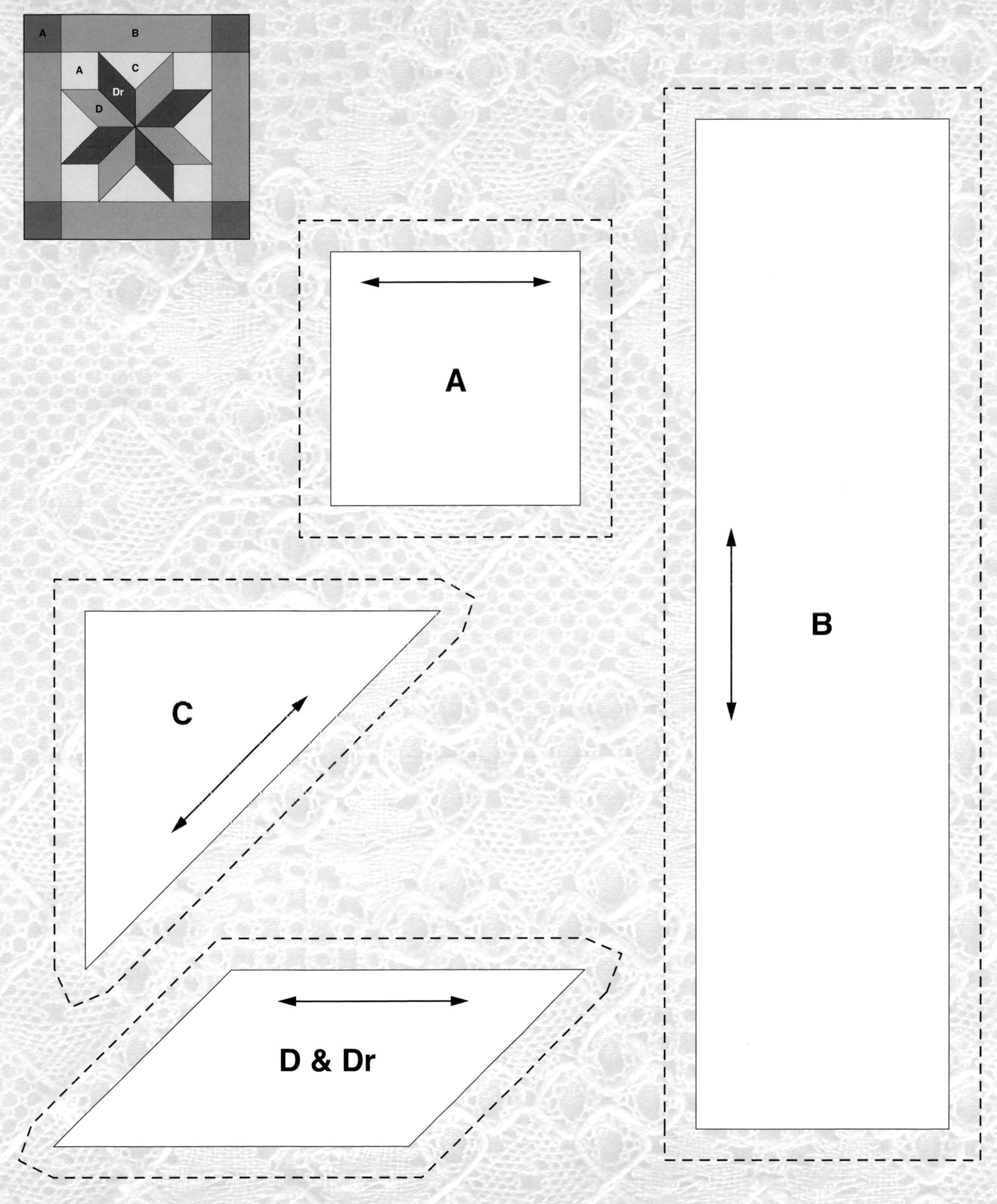
A
B
A
C
Dr
D
A
B
C
D & Dr

Sparkling jewels, pearls of wisdom sparkling jewels,
pearls of wisdom sparkling jewels, pearls of wisdom
sparkling jewels, pearls of wisdom sparkling jewels,

kling jewels, pearls of wisdom
of wisdom sparkling jewels,
kling jewels, pearls of wisdom
of wisdom sparkling jewels,
kling jewels, pearls of wisdom
of wisdom sparkling jewels,
kling jewels, pearls of wisdom
of wisdom sparkling jewels,
kling jewels, pearls of wisdom
of wisdom sparkling jewels,
kling jewels, pearls of wisdom
sparkling jewels, pearls of wisdom sparkling jewels,
pearls of wisdom sparkling jewels, pearls of wisdom
sparkling jewels, pearls of wisdom sparkling jewels,

Diamond Cross

DIAMOND CROSS

Made by Rosemary Garten, Independence, Missouri.

DIAMOND CROSS

12" block

You will need to make two of these blocks for the quilt.

For EACH block, cut:

- 4 scant 2" squares (template A), 2 – 3 7/16" squares (template E) and 1 - 3 1/2" x 9 5/16" (template C) rectangle from the medium-light fabric

- 8 scant 2" squares (template A) from dark fabric

- 4 - 2 3/8" squares (or cut 8 triangles using template D) and 8 – 2" x 4 15/16" strips (template B and Br) from the background fabric. To get the reverse pieces, fold the fabric, right sides together and cut through two layers at once. Use the template to cut the angle for the B and Br pieces.

- 8 – 2 3/8" squares using the medium fabric. Recut 4 of the 2 3/8" squares from corner to corner making 8 triangles (template D).

You will need to make 8 half-square triangle units using the 2 3/8" squares of background fabric and medium fabric. To make the units, draw a line from corner to corner on the diagonal on the reverse side of the background squares. Place a background square atop a medium square with right sides facing. Sew 1/4" on both sides of the line. Cut the units apart on the line using your rotary cutter and ruler. If using the B templates, sew the triangles together. Press the units open toward the darker fabric.

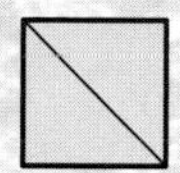
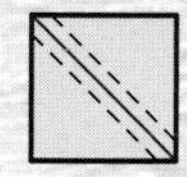

Make four 4-patch units by sewing a dark square to a half-square triangle unit as shown. Then sew a half-square triangle unit to a dark square. Sew the two units together as shown. Remember, you need to make four of these units per block.

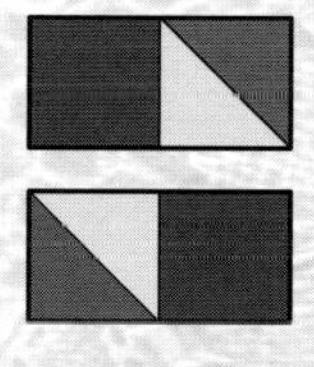
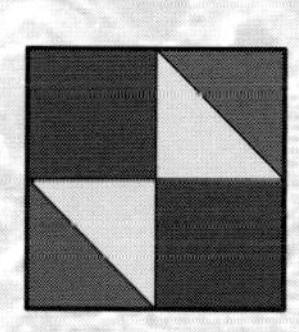

Sew a 4-patch unit to opposite sides of each E square. You should end up with two strips that look like this.

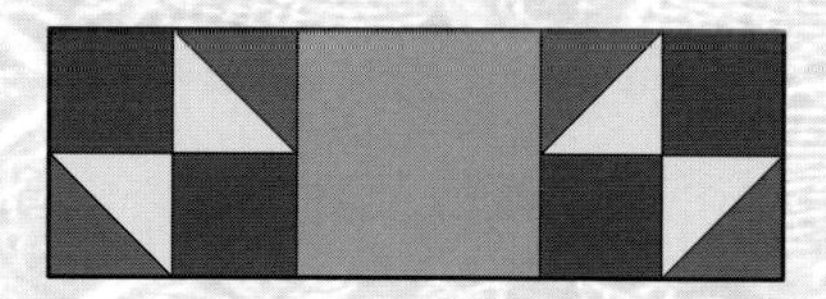

Sew one of these strips to each long side of the center C strip as shown.

Now sew the D triangles to the B and Br strips. Sew the B and Br strips together. You should have four strips that look like this.

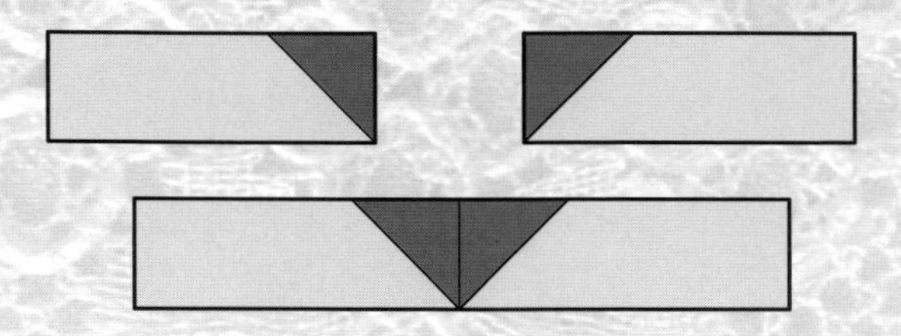

Sew an A square to each end of two of the strips.

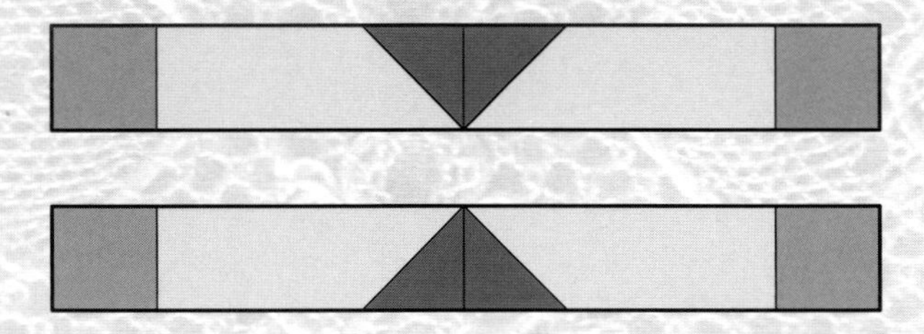

Now stitch a B and Br strip to each side of the center of the block.

Add the two strips that have the A squares at the ends to the top and bottom of the block to complete it.

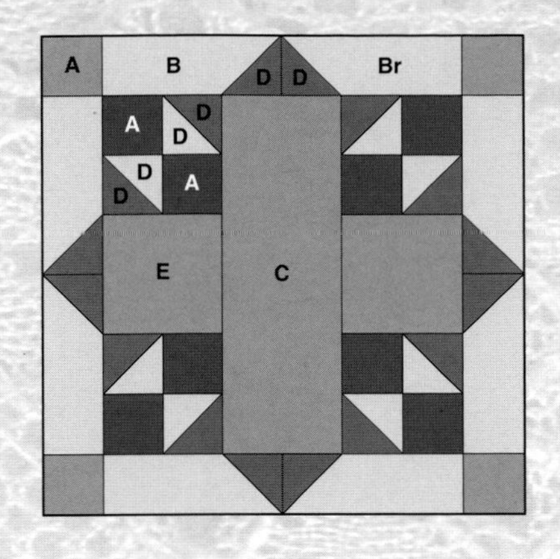
A
B
D
D
Br
A
D
D
D
D
A
E
C

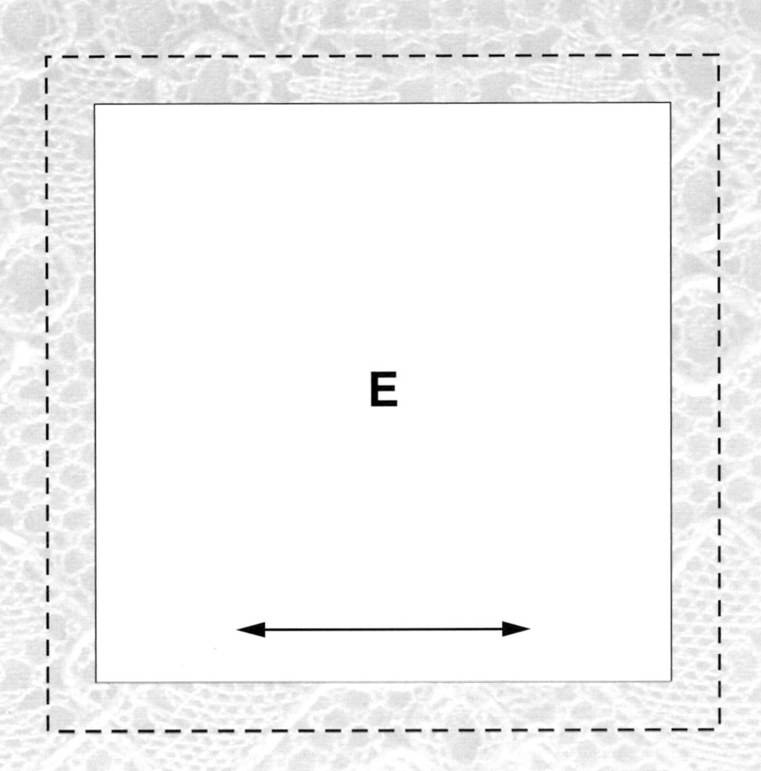
E

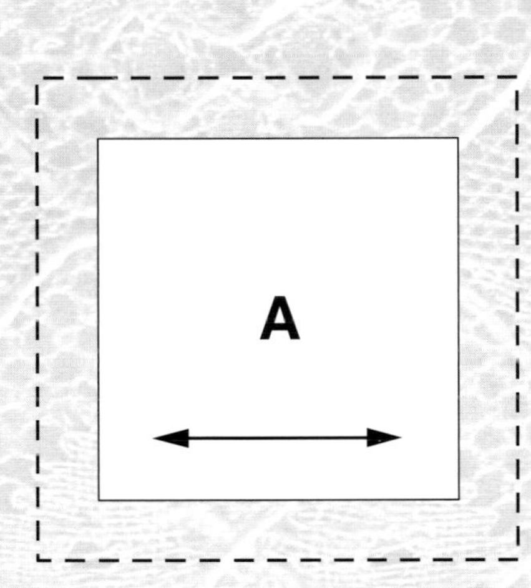
A

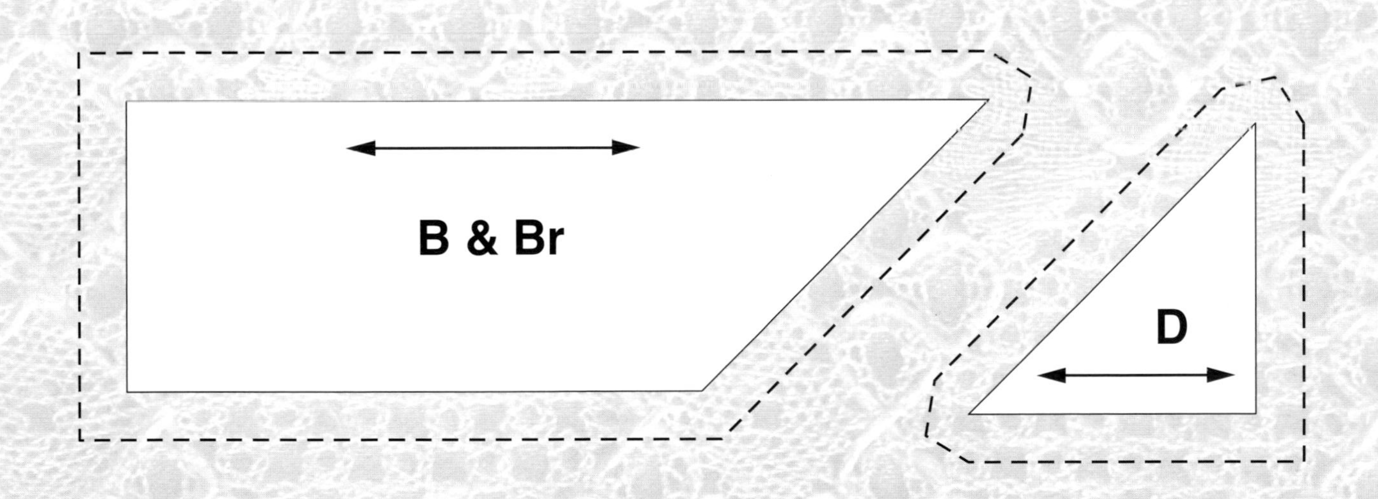
B & Br
D

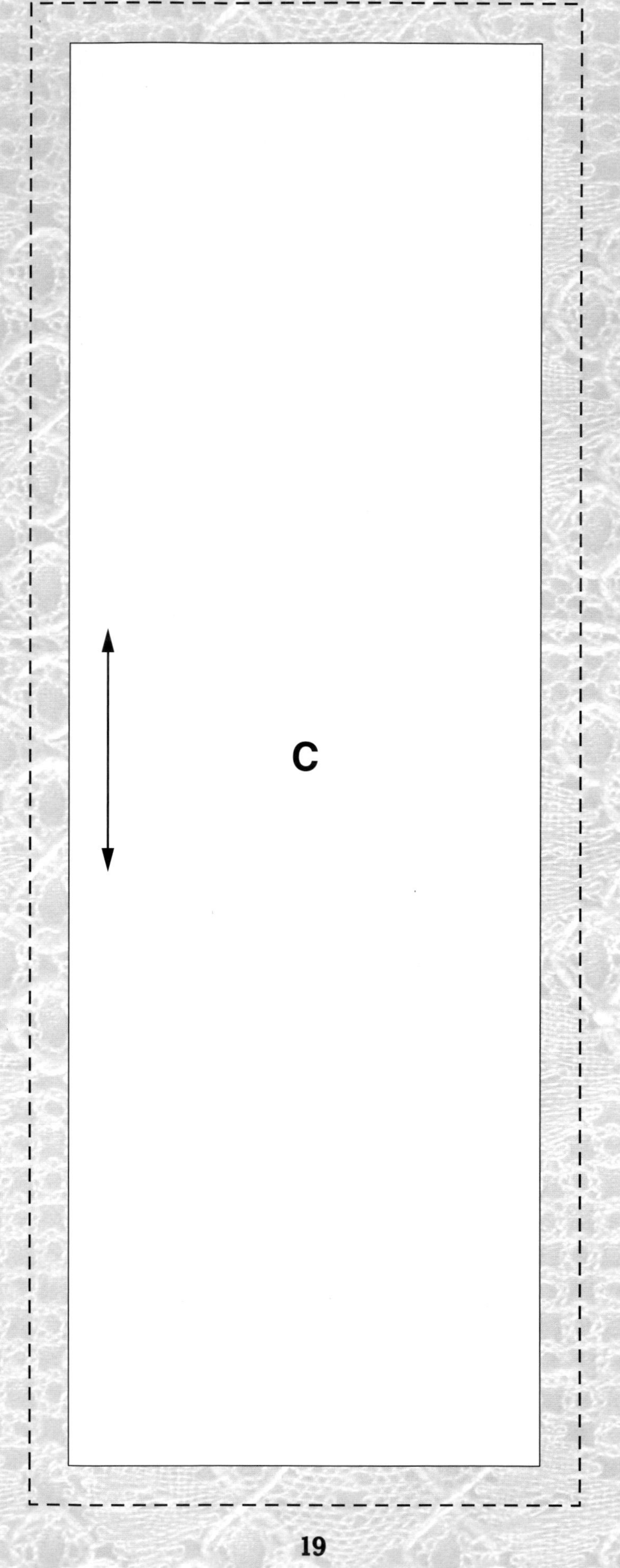
C

Flash of Diamonds

FLASH OF DIAMONDS

Made by Peggy and Corky Hutinett, Raytown, Missouri.

FLASH OF DIAMONDS

12" block

You will need to make two of these blocks for the quilt.

For EACH block, cut:

- 12 diamonds using template C from the dark fabric

- 12 diamonds using template C from the medium fabric

- 1 - 7 1/4" square using medium light fabric. Cut the square from corner to corner on both diagonals making quarter square triangles (template D).

From background fabric:

- 8 – squares using template A. (The square measures 2 9/32". Since this is such an odd measurement, you might just want to cut a paper template, place it on the fabric and cut, using the template as a guide.)

- 4 – 2 5/8" squares. Cut the squares from corner to corner on the diagonal into 8 triangles (template B). If you use template B, make sure the grain lines of the fabric run with the short edges of the triangles.

- 3 – 3 3/4" squares. Cut these squares from corner to corner on each diagonal, making quarter square triangles (template B). NOTE: if you are using template B, make sure the grain of the fabric runs across the widest part of the triangle. This way the straight of grain will be on the outer edge of the block.

Begin by piecing the center section of the block. Sew a dark diamond to the left side of a B triangle. Add a medium diamond to the right side of the triangle. As soon as you hit the seam line, stop and take a couple of back stitches. DO NOT SEW INTO THE SEAM LINE. If you are not sure where to stop sewing, mark all your pieces with a dot where the seams intersect. You can do this by punching a hole in each corner of your template with a 1/8" punch. Make 4 of these units.

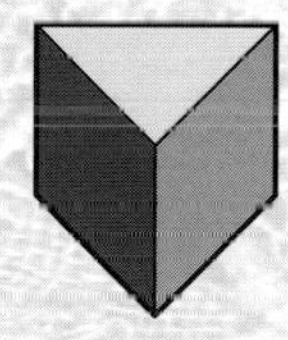

Now add an A square to each of the units. Do not sew into the seam line. They should now look like this.

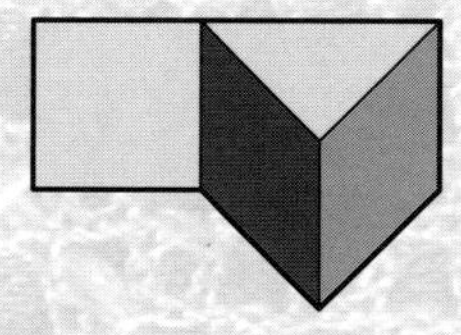

To join the units, sew two pairs of diamonds that have the squares attached to make half of the star. Do this twice, then sew the two together. If you are piecing this on your sewing machine, set it on the longest stitch. Baste a couple of stitches at the beginning of the seam. Raise your presser foot and move to the first part of the star that meets and add a couple of basting stitches at that point. Then move onto the center and baste a few stitches. Go on to the last point where the star meets and baste again and finally baste at the end of the seam line. Open up the block. Check to make sure all your points match. Reset your machine and sew the seams together if you're happy with the points.

Make the four corner units next by sewing a dark diamond to a B triangle. Add a medium diamond to the triangle and add a B triangle to the medium diamond. The next portion is the same but is a mirror image. Add the A background square and join the two sections together. Set these units aside for the moment.

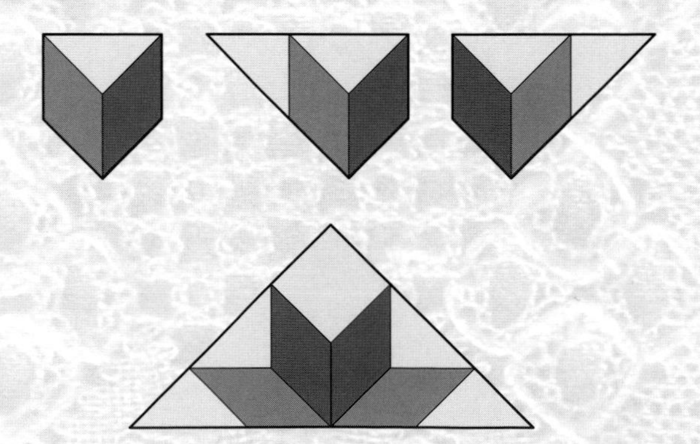

Go back to the center portion of your block. Add the large D triangles as shown.

Finish the block by adding the four corner units. Your block should now look like this.

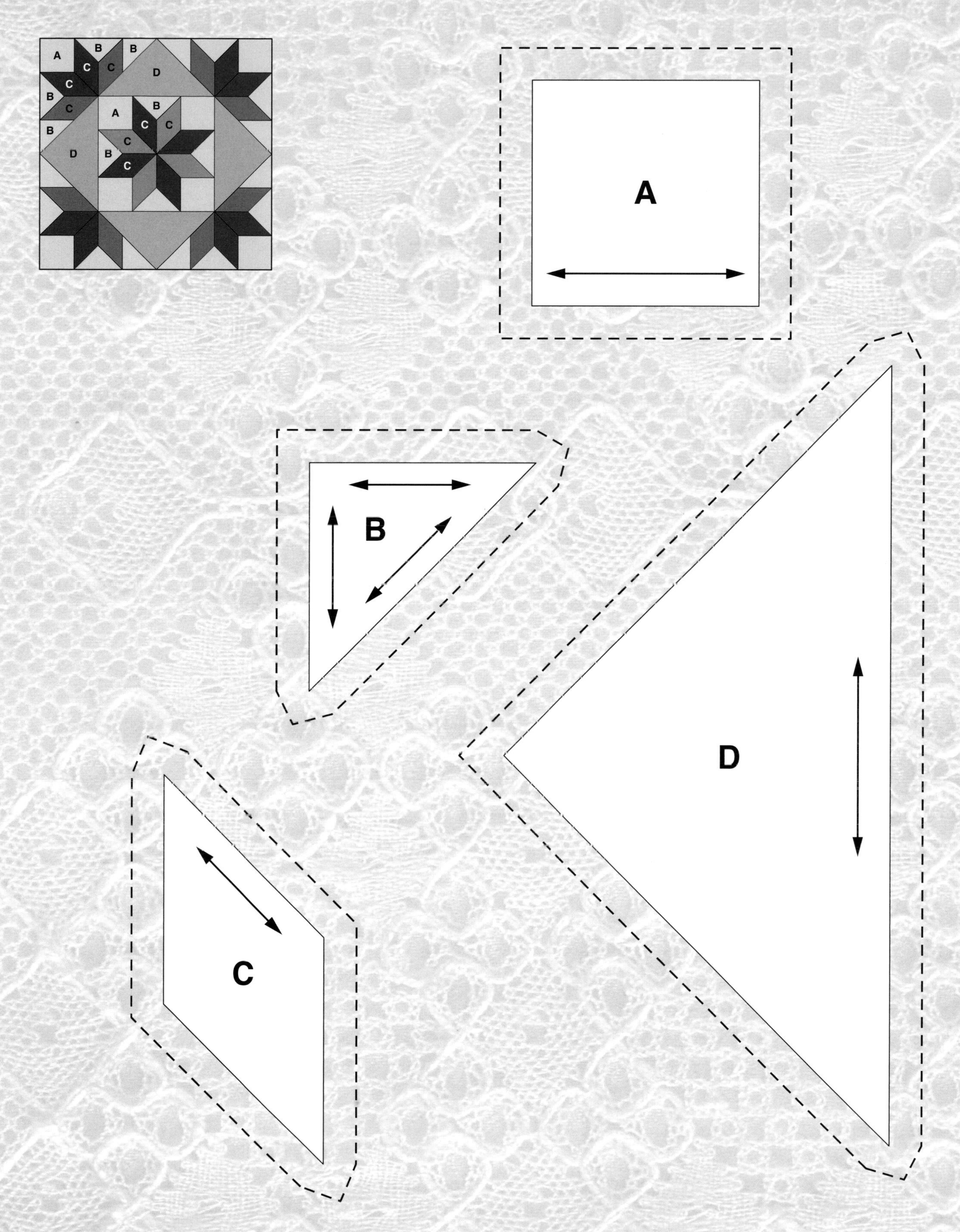
A
B
C
D

Sparkling jewels, pearls of wisdom sparkling jewels,
pearls of wisdom sparkling jewels, pearls of wisdom
sparkling jewels, pearls of wisdom sparkling jewels,
pearls of wisdom sparkling jewels, pearls of wisdom
om sparkling jewels,
els, pearls of wisdom
om sparkling jewels,
els, pearls of wisdom
om sparkling jewels,
els, pearls of wisdom
om sparkling jewels,
els, pearls of wisdom
om sparkling jewels,
els, pearls of wisdom
om sparkling jewels,
pearls of wisdom sparkling jewels, pearls of wisdom
sparkling jewels, pearls of wisdom sparkling jewels,

Frame with Diamonds

FRAME WITH DIAMONDS
Made by Rosemary Garten and Judy Lovell.

FRAME WITH DIAMONDS

12" Block

Because this is such a difficult block to piece, I have changed it to a paper pieced pattern. You will need to make eight of these blocks for the quilt.

You will need to make four of each of the units per block. You will then sew the units together to make the block. In unit A and unit C, the medium fabric goes in position 1. The dark fabric goes in positions 2 and 3 and the background fabric goes in position 4. In units B and D, background fabric goes in position 1 and dark fabric goes in positions 2 and 3.

Sew unit A to unit B, then sew unit C to unit D. Join the two units together by sewing the two angles together. You need four of these per block.

Wait until the blocks are all sewn together and the quilt top is complete to tear off the paper.

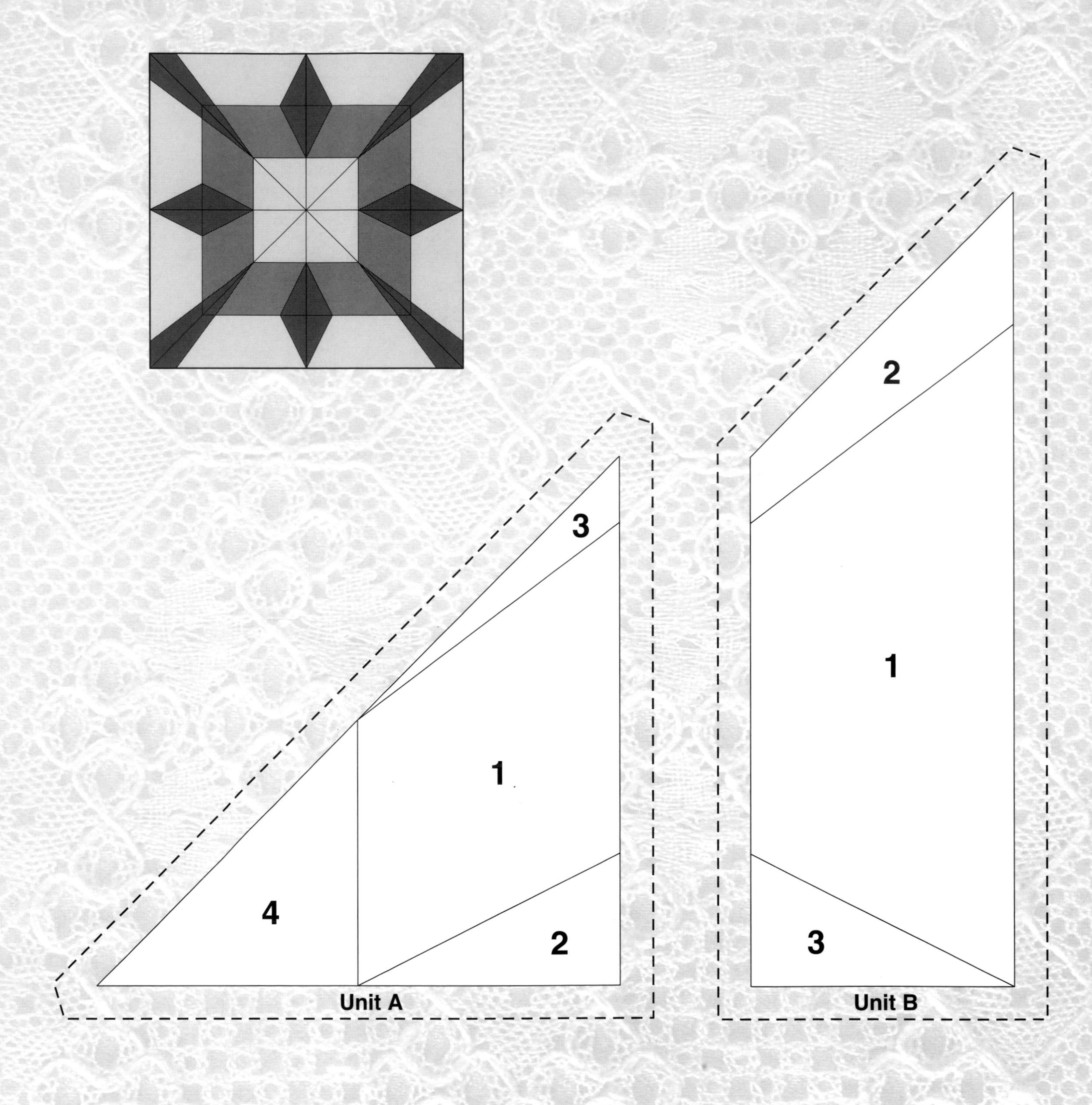
3
1
4
2
Unit A
2
1
3
Unit B

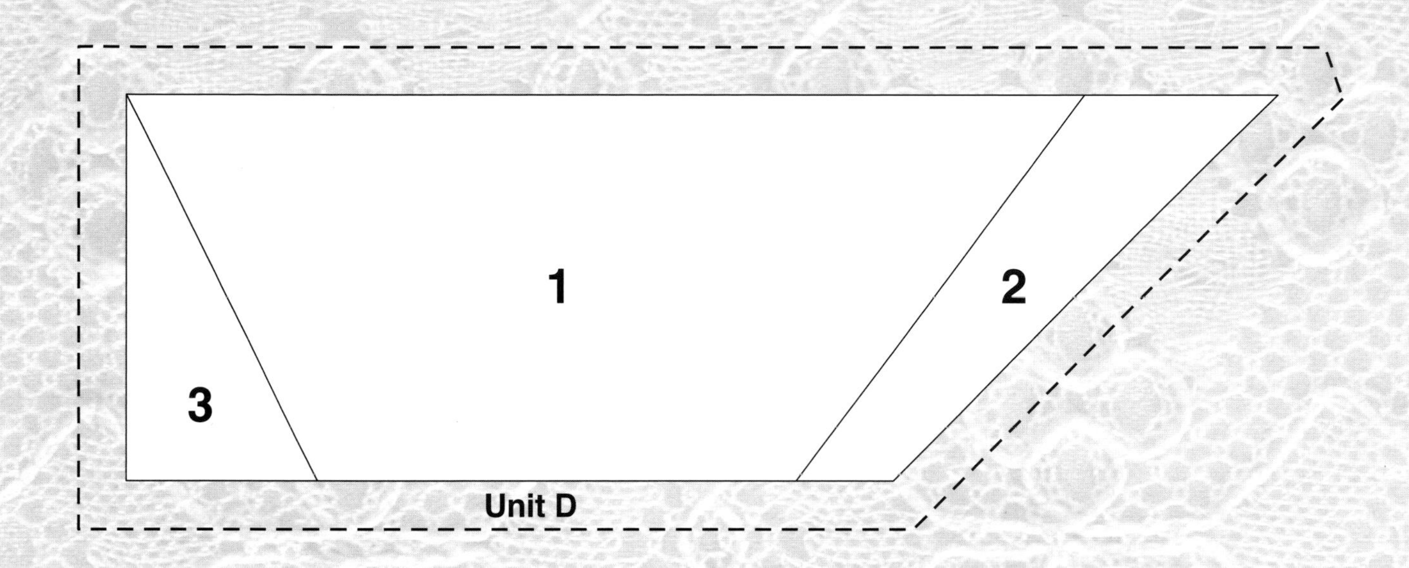
1
2
3
Unit D

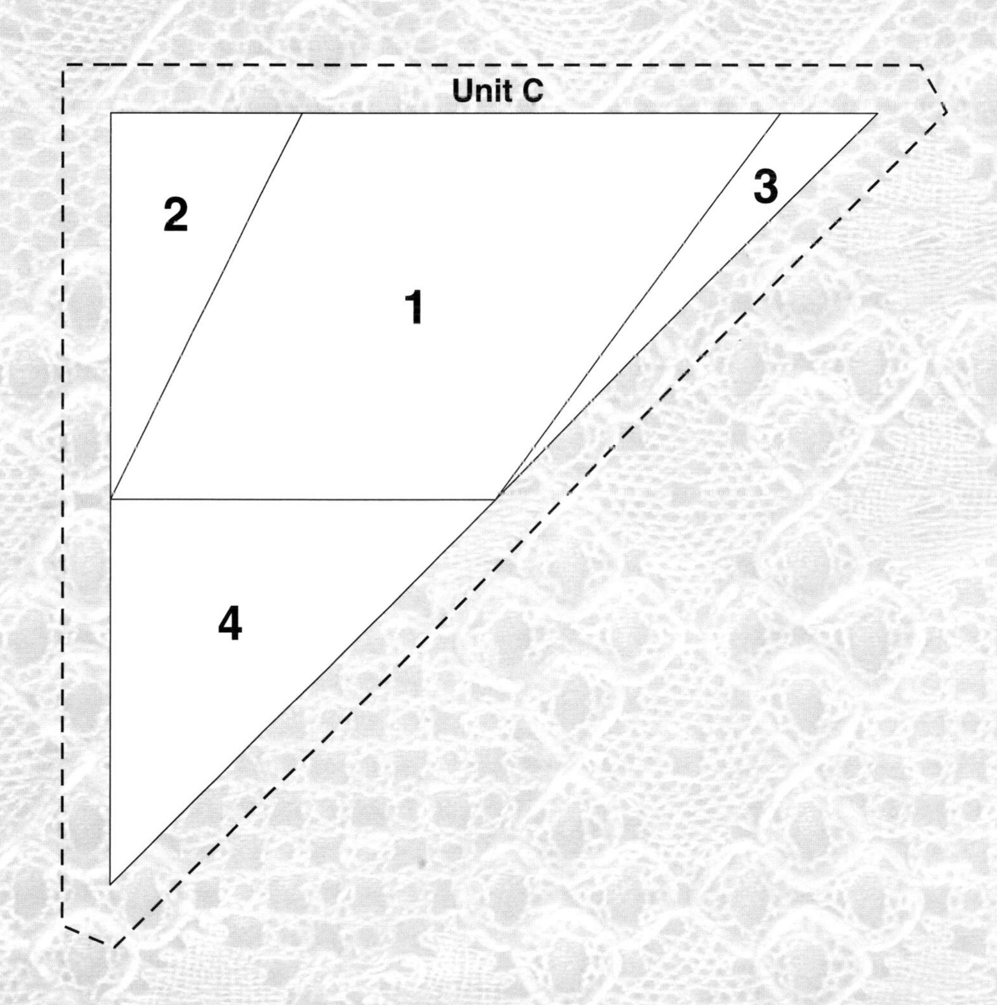
Unit C
2
3
1
4

Sparkling jewels, pearls of wisdom sparkling jewels,

pearls of wisdom sparkling jewels, pearls of wisdom

sparkling jewels, pearls of wisdom sparkling jewels,

pearls of wisdom sparkling jewels, pearls of wisdom

sparkling jewels, pearls of wisdom sparkling jewels,

els, pearls of wisdom

om sparkling jewels,

els, pearls of wisdom

om sparkling jewels,

els, pearls of wisdom

om sparkling jewels,

els, pearls of wisdom

om sparkling jewels,

els, pearls of wisdom

om sparkling jewels,

pearls of wisdom sparkling jewels, pearls of wisdom

sparkling jewels, pearls of wisdom sparkling jewels,

Grandma's Brooch

GRANDMA'S BROOCH

Made by Judy Lovell, Independence, Missouri.

GRANDMA'S BROOCH

12" block

You will need to make two of these blocks for the quilt.

For EACH block, cut:

- 8 – 3" squares (template C) from a medium color, and
- 2 – 4 3/8" squares cut on the diagonal from corner to corner to make 4 triangles (template A)
- 8 – diamonds using template B from the background fabric
- 12 – triangles using template D from the dark fabric
- 4 – triangles using template D from the background fabric

Sew the 4 center D triangles together, alternating the dark and medium-light colors. Make two, then sew the two halves together. Set aside for the moment.

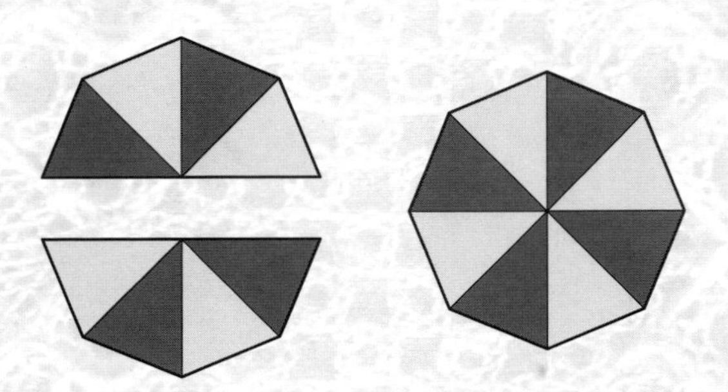

Sew the long side of two D triangles to two adjacent sides of a C square as shown. Make four of these units. DO NOT SEW INTO THE SEAM ALLOWANCE at the beginning or the end of the unit.

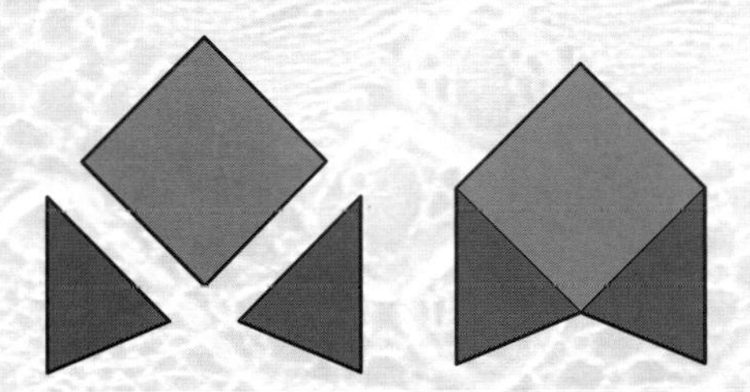

Add a medium C square to two sides of two of the DCD units.

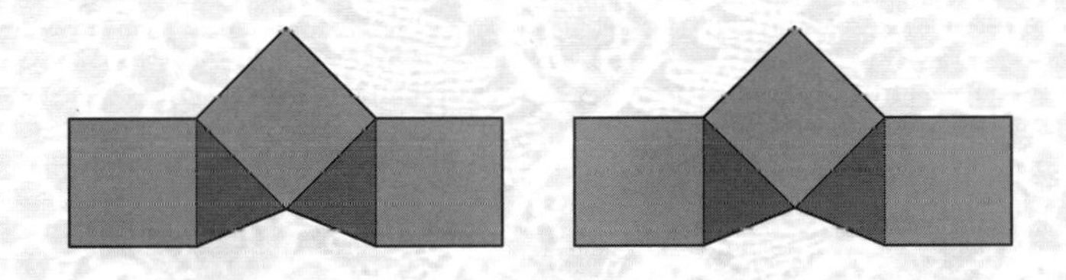

Sew a DCD unit to opposing sides of the center triangles.

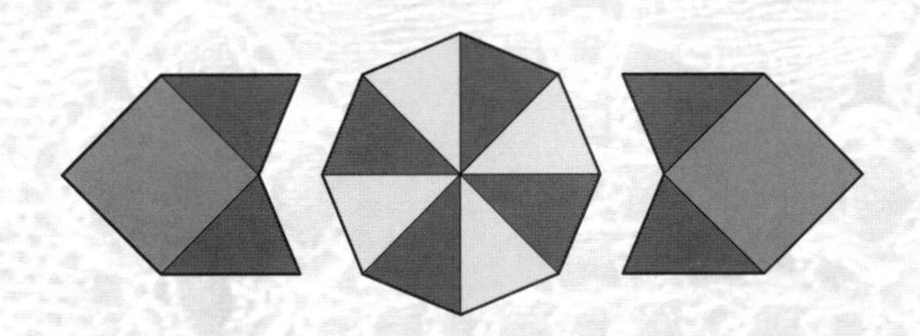

Now add the DCD units that have the squares sewn onto the top and bottom of the center. Your block should now look like this.

Complete the block by adding the four A triangles to the corners.

Add the background B diamonds.

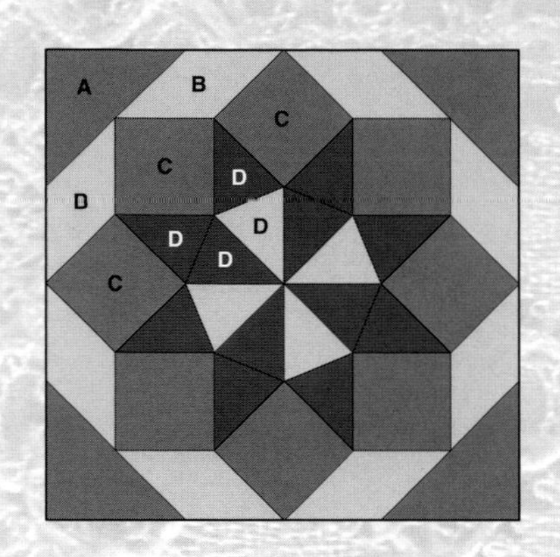
A
B
C
C
D
B
D
D
D
C

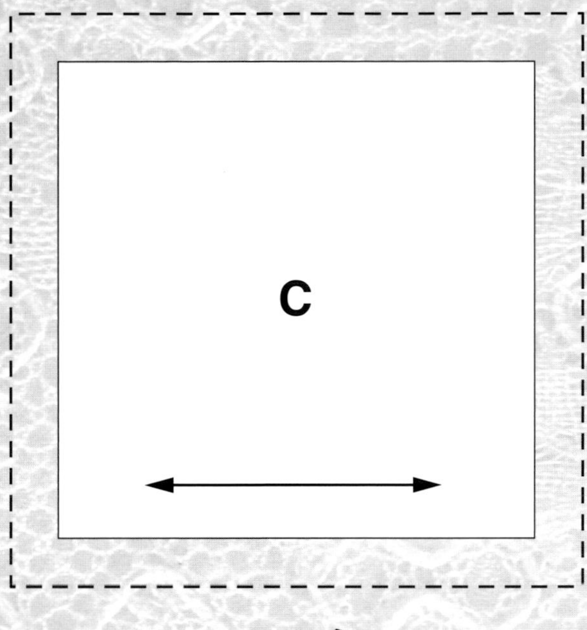
C

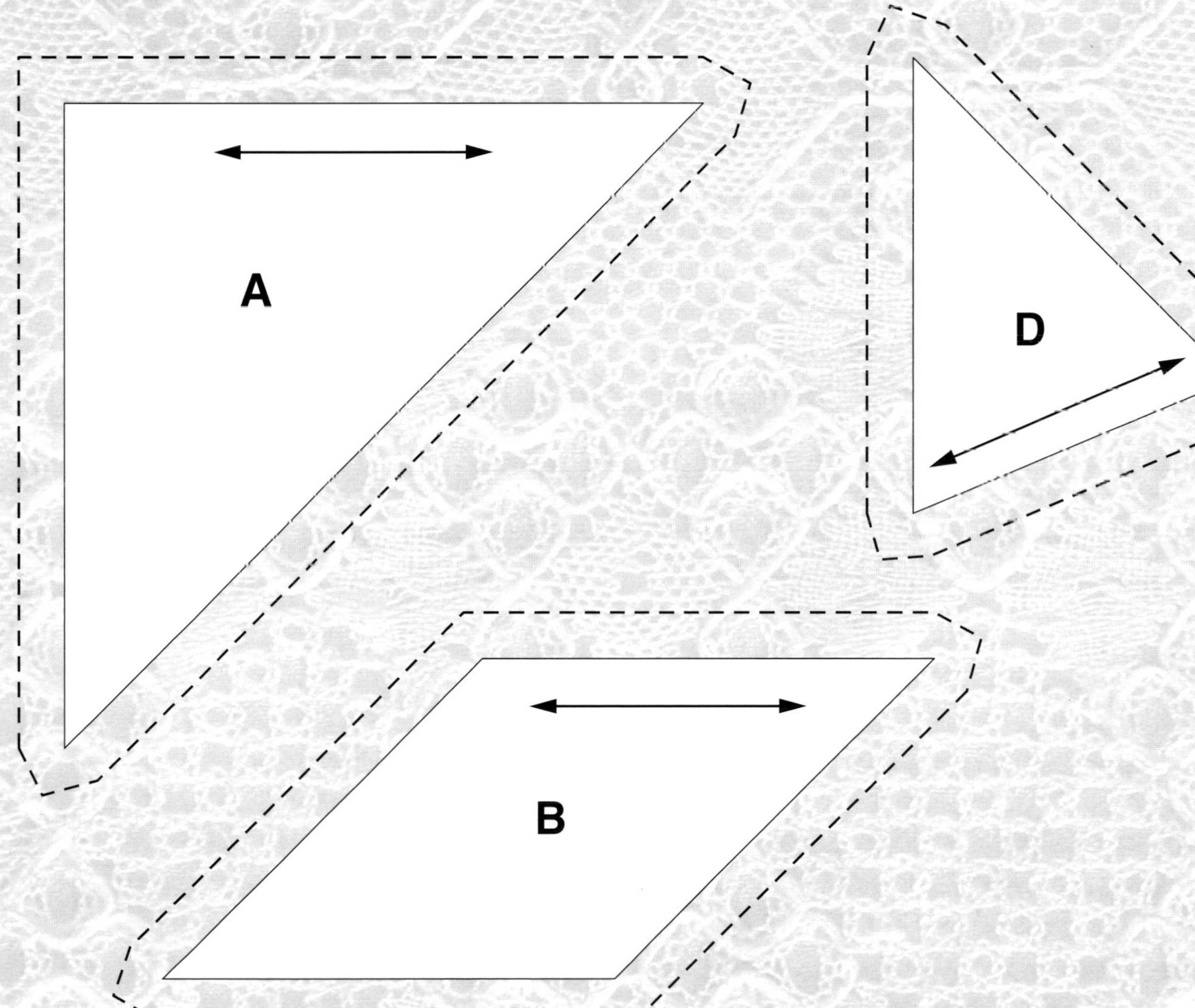
A
D
B

Sparkling jewels, pearls of wisdom sparkling jewels,

pearls of wisdom sparkling jewels, pearls of wisdom

sparkling jewels, pearls of wisdom sparkling jewels,

pearls of wisdom sparkling jewels, pearls of wisdom

isdom sparkling jewels,

jewels, pearls of wisdom

isdom sparkling jewels,

jewels, pearls of wisdom

isdom sparkling jewels,

jewels, pearls of wisdom

isdom sparkling jewels,

jewels, pearls of wisdom

isdom sparkling jewels,

jewels, pearls of wisdom

isdom sparkling jewels,

pearls of wisdom sparkling jewels, pearls of wisdom

sparkling jewels, pearls of wisdom sparkling jewels,

Jewels in a Frame

JEWELS IN A FRAME
Made by Linda Kriesel, Independence, Missouri.

JEWELS IN A FRAME

12" block

For the quilt, you will need to make eight of these blocks.

For EACH block, cut:

- 4 – A triangles and 24 – B triangles from the background fabric. NOTE: When cutting the B triangles, make sure the straight of grain of the fabric runs parallel to the long edge of the triangle.
- 8 – pieces using template D and 4 C diamonds from the dark fabric
- 12 – C diamonds from the medium fabric

To make the center portion of the block, sew a dark C diamond to the right side of a B triangle. Add a medium C diamond to the left side of the triangle. Make four of these units. Sew a B triangle to opposing sides of two of the diamond units as shown.

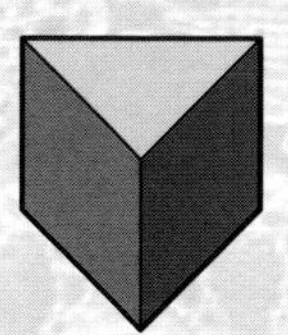

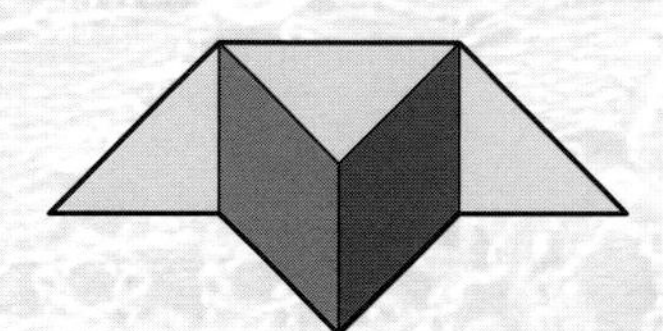

Now sew a diamond unit to each. You now have two halves. Finger press all the seams going in the same direction so the center will come together properly in the next step.

Readjust your stitch length to a basting stitch. Baste the two halves together taking a few stitches wherever your seams and points meet. Open your block up and check to see if everything matches. If you are happy with your results, shorten your stitches and sew the two halves together.

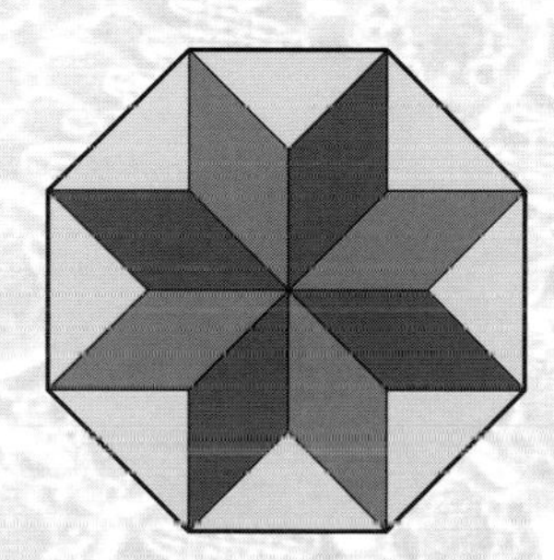

Now we need to build the units for the outer portion of the block. Sew a diamond to the left side of a B triangle. Add a D piece to the right side of the triangle. Remember, do not sew into the quarter-inch seam allowance. If necessary, mark your seam allowances on your pieces. Since the seam allowances will not be crossed at the beginning and the end of the seams, you need to lock your stitches. To do this, shorten your stitch length rather than trying to backstitch.This is also a great place to use your pinning techniques. There are a lot of bias edges in this block and you don't want your pieces to skew.

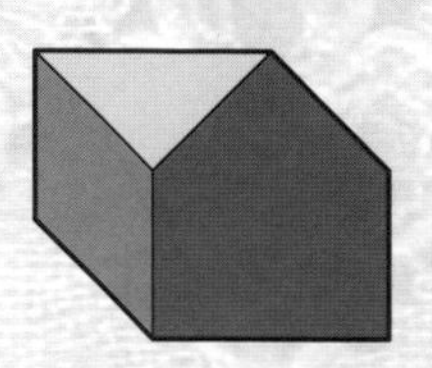

Add another B triangle and diamond as shown. Make four of these.

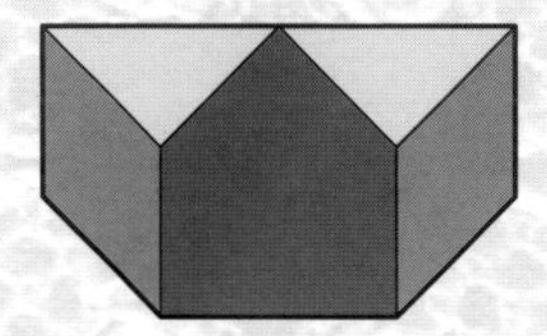

Sew a B triangle to both sides of the remaining D pieces.

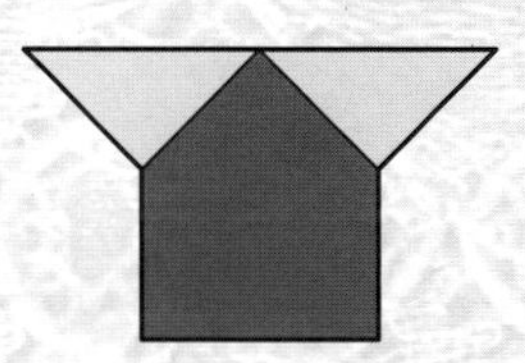

Attach the units to the center star as shown.

Sew on the four corner A triangles to complete the block.

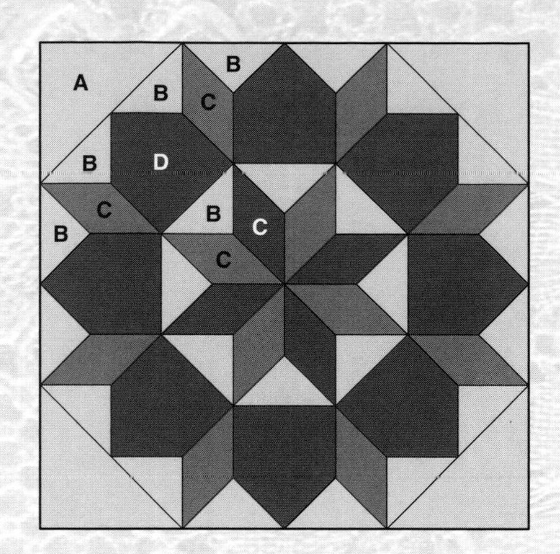
A
B
B
C
B
D
C
B
B
C
C

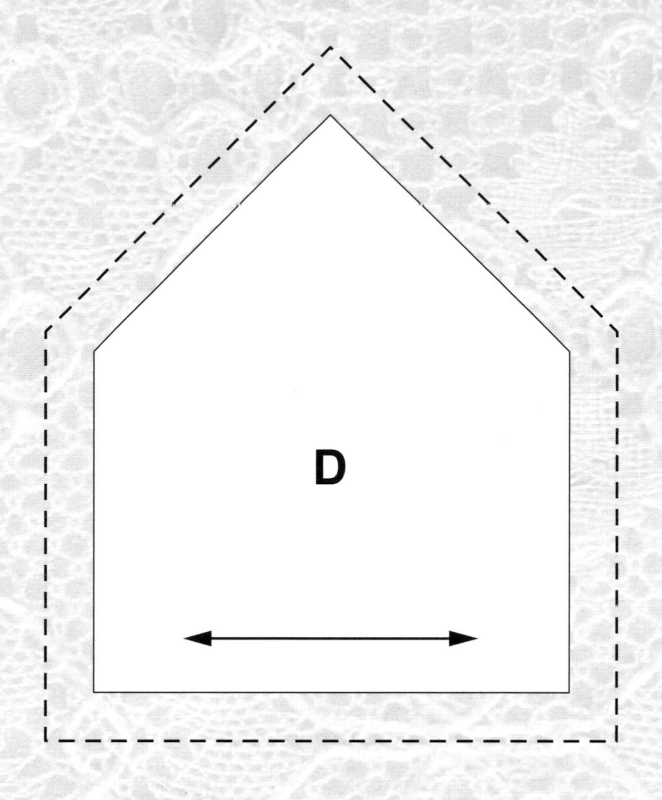
D

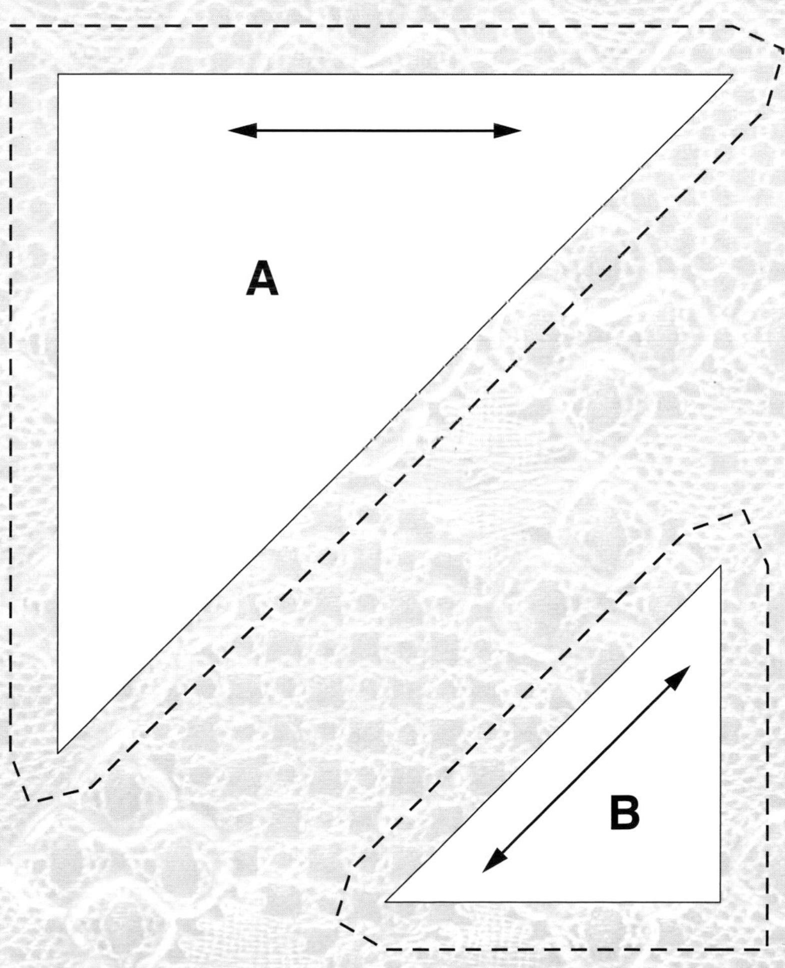
A
B

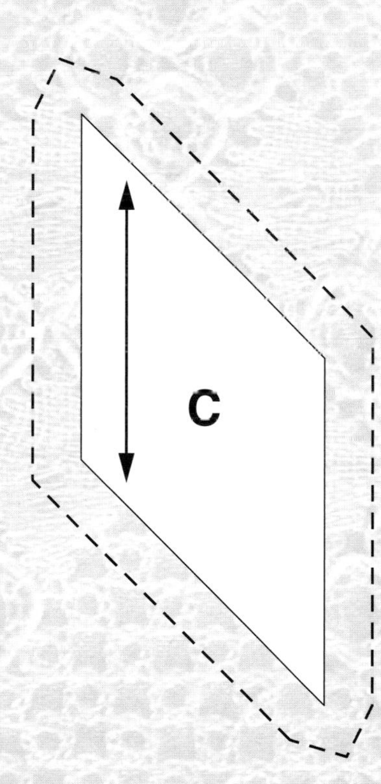
C

Sparkling jewels, pearls of wisdom sparkling jewels,
pearls of wisdom sparkling jewels, pearls of wisdom
sparkling jewels, pearls of wisdom sparkling jewels,
pearls of wisdom sparkling jewels, pearls of wisdom

m sparkling jewels,
ls, pearls of wisdom
m sparkling jewels,
ls, pearls of wisdom
m sparkling jewels,
ls, pearls of wisdom
m sparkling jewels,
ls, pearls of wisdom
m sparkling jewels,
ls, pearls of wisdom
m sparkling jewels,

pearls of wisdom sparkling jewels, pearls of wisdom
sparkling jewels, pearls of wisdom sparkling jewels,

Squares and Diamonds

SQUARES AND DIAMONDS
Made by Brenda Butcher, Independence, Missouri.

SQUARES AND DIAMONDS

12" block

You must make two of these blocks for the quilt.

For EACH block, cut

- 2 – 4 7/8" squares from the background fabric (or use template A to cut 4 triangles)
- 2 – 4 7/8" squares from the medium light fabric (or use template A to cut 4 triangles)
- 2 – 5 1/4" squares from the medium light fabric (or use template B to cut 8 B triangles)
- 1 – 2 1/2" square (template D) from the medium light fabric
- 4 – 4 1/2" x 1 1/2" rectangles (template C) from the dark fabric
- 2 – 5 1/4" squares from the dark fabric (or use template B to cut 8 B triangles)

You will need to make four half-square triangles for this set of blocks. To do so, draw a diagonal line from corner to corner on the reverse side of the two 4 7/8" background squares. Place each light square atop a medium light square with right sides facing and sew 1/4" on both sides of the line. Using your rotary cutter and ruler, cut along the line. Open each half-square triangle unit and press toward the darker fabric. (Of course, if you are using the templates, sew a light A triangle to a medium light A triangle. Make 4 half square triangles.)

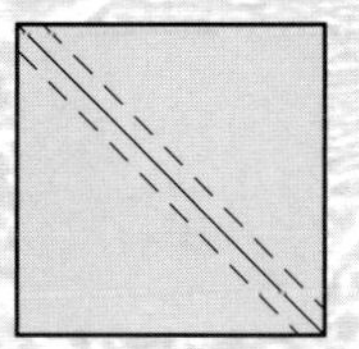

Now you need to make four quarter-square triangle units. To do this, draw a line from corner to corner on the diagonal of the two 5 1/4" squares of medium light fabric. Place a medium square atop a dark square and sew 1/4" on both sides of the line. Using your rotary cutter, cut the units apart on the line. You now have half-square triangles. Draw a line from corner to corner on four of the half-square triangle units, intersecting the seam line. Place one half-square triangle unit atop the other with right sides facing, making sure you have turned one of the squares. Sew 1/4" on both sides of the line. Cut on the line using your rotary cutter to separate the units. You should have four units that look like this. (If using the templates, cut 8 B triangles from the dark fabric and 8 B triangles from the medium light fabric. Sew the units together as shown in the diagram.)

Using your C template, miter the ends of the four C strips. Sew two C strips to opposite sides of the D square first. Start and stop 1/4" from the edge. Add the remaining two strips to the top and bottom. Sew the angles last.

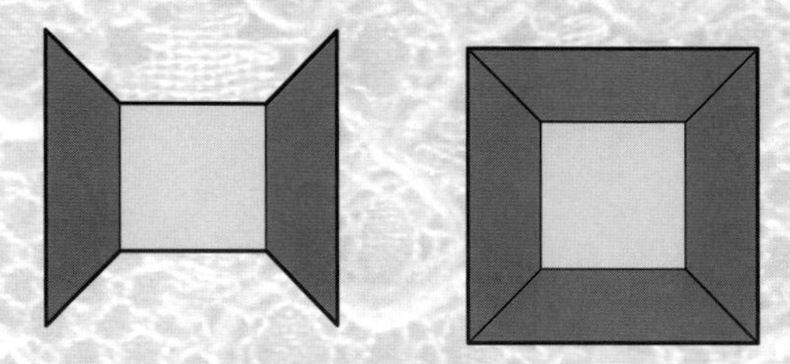

You are now ready to construct the block. Sew two half-square triangle units to opposite sides of a quarter-square triangle unit. Make two strips like this.

Sew a quarter-square triangle unit to opposite sides of the center square.

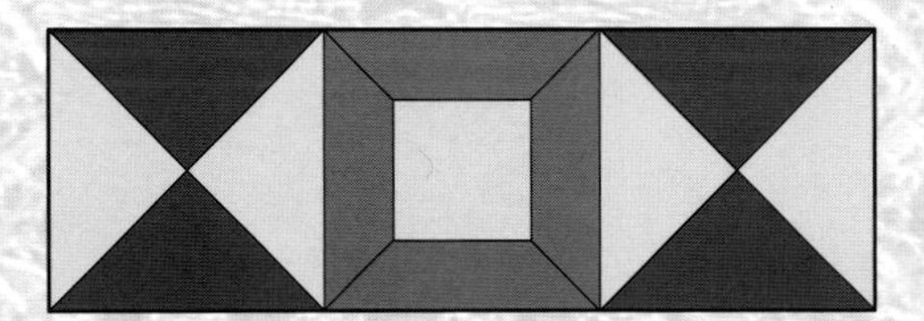

Sew the three rows together to complete the block.

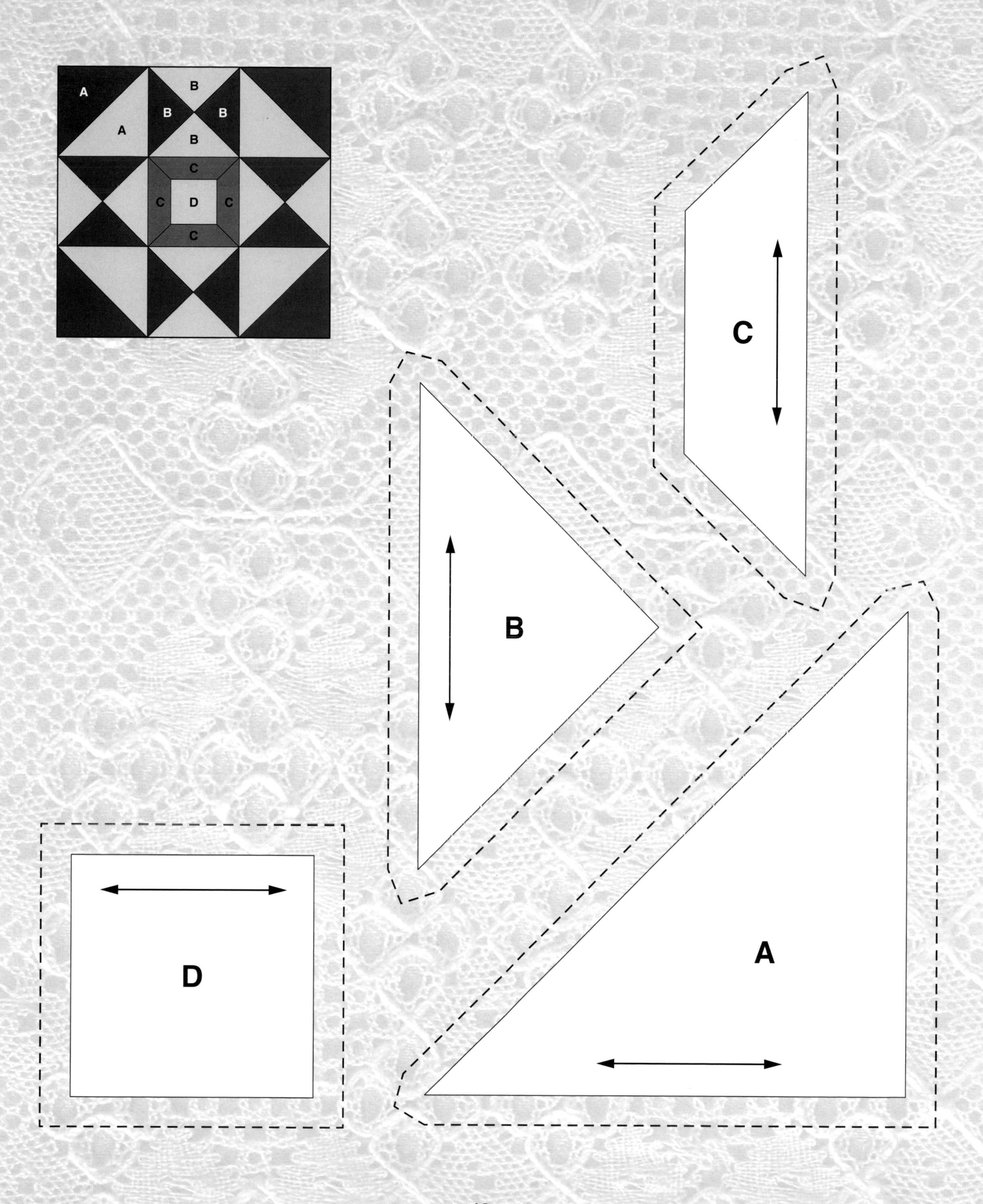
A
A
B
B
B
B
C
C
D
C
C
C
B
D
A

Sparkling jewels, pearls of wisdom sparkling jewels,
pearls of wisdom sparkling jewels, pearls of wisdom
sparkling jewels, pearls of wisdom sparkling jewels,
pearls of wisdom sparkling jewels, pearls of wisdom
sparkling jewels, pearls of wisdom sparkling jewels,
pearls of wisdom sparkling jewels, pearls of wisdom
wisdom sparkling jewels,
ng jewels, pearls of wisdom
wisdom sparkling jewels,
ng jewels, pearls of wisdom
wisdom sparkling jewels,
ng jewels, pearls of wisdom
wisdom sparkling jewels,
ng jewels, pearls of wisdom
wisdom sparkling jewels,
ng jewels, pearls of wisdom
sparkling jewels, pearls of wisdom sparkling jewels,

Star of Diamond Points

STAR OF DIAMOND POINTS
Made by Margaret Falen, Grain Valley, Missouri.

STAR OF DIAMOND POINTS

12" block

You will need to make two of these blocks for the quilt.

For EACH block, cut:

- 4 diamonds using template C from the dark fabric
- 4 diamonds using template C from the medium light fabric
- 1 - 6 1/4" square using background fabric. Cut the square from corner to corner on both diagonals making quarter-square triangles (or cut four triangles using template B).
- 4 – 4" squares (template A) from background fabric

Sew a medium diamond to the left side of a B triangle. Add a dark diamond to the right side of the triangle. As soon as you hit the seam line, stop and lock your stitches. DO NOT SEW INTO THE SEAM LINE. If you are not sure where to stop sewing, mark all your pieces with a dot where the seams intersect. You can do this by punching a hole in each corner of your template with a 1/8" punch. Make 4 of these units.

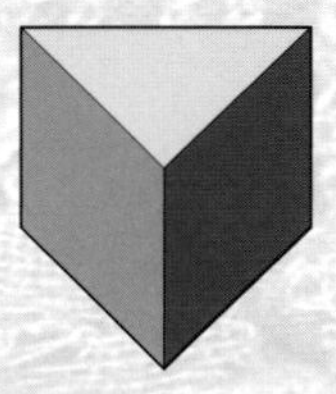

Now add an A square to the left side of each unit. Do not sew into the seam line. They should now look like this.

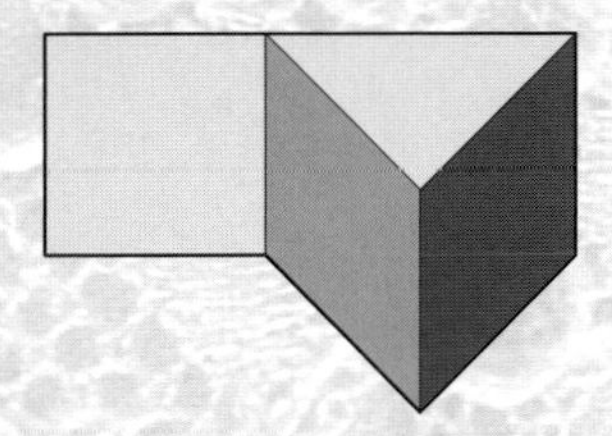

To join the units, sew two pairs of diamonds that have the squares attached to make half of the star. Do this twice then sew the two together. Set your sewing machine on the longest stitch. Baste a couple of stitches at the beginning of the seam. Raise your presser foot and move to the first part of the star that meets and add a couple of basting stitches at that point. Then move onto the center and baste a few stitches. Go on to the last point where the star meets and baste again and finally baste at the end of the seam line. Open up the block. Check to make sure all your points match. Reset your machine stitch length and sew the seams together if you're happy with the points.

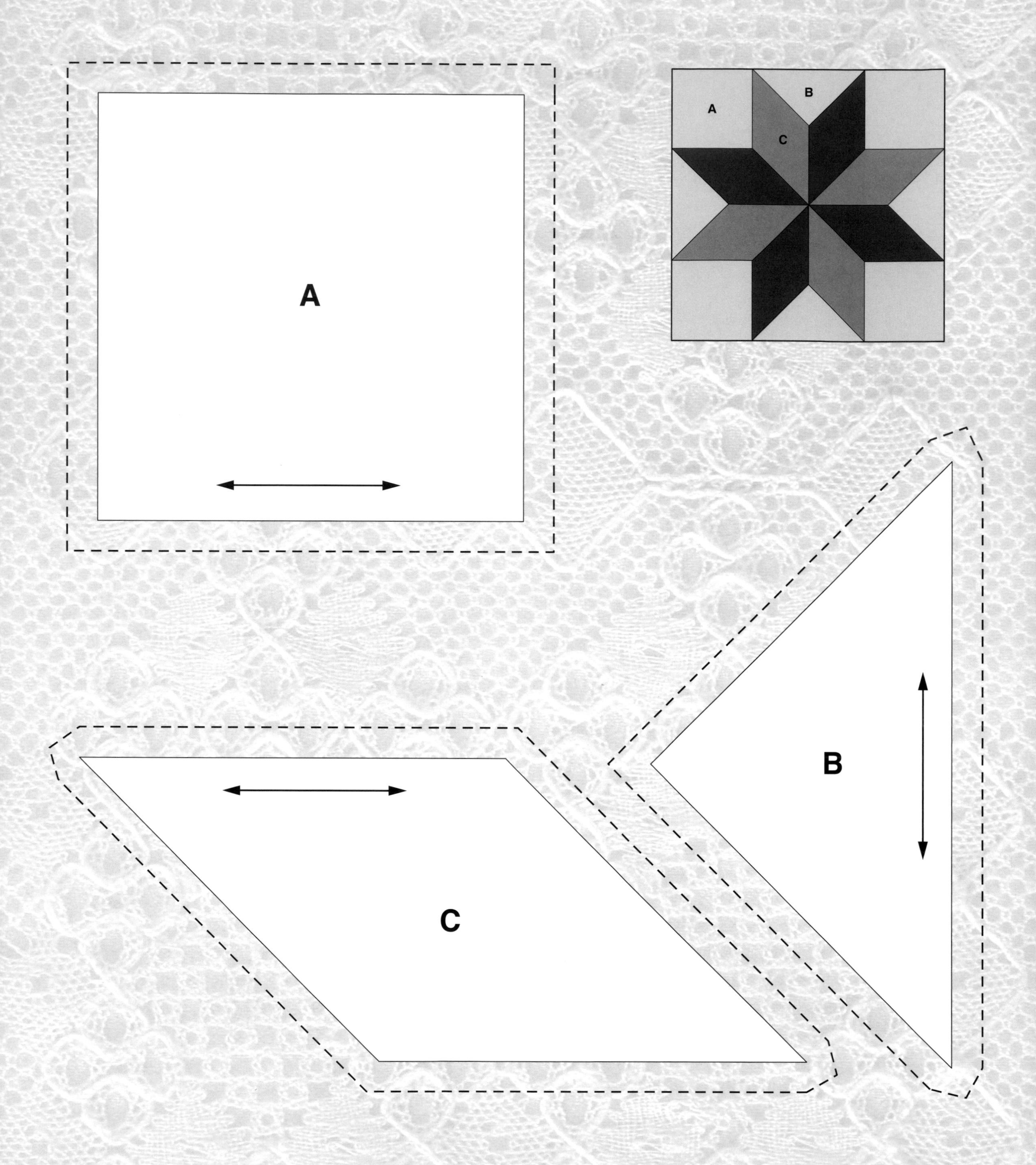
A
B
C
A
B
C

The Square Diamond

THE SQUARE DIAMOND

Made by Judy Hill, Independence, Missouri.

THE SQUARE DIAMOND

12" block

You will need to make two of these blocks for the quilt.

For EACH block,

From the background fabric, cut

- 4 – 12 1/2" x 1 1/2" strips (template A)
- 1 - 2 5/8" square (template F)
- 2 – 3 3/8" squares (or four triangles using template D)

From the medium fabric, cut

- 8 – 5 1/2" x 1 1/2" strips (template C)

From the medium light fabric, cut

- 2 – 3 3/8" squares (or four triangles using template D)
- 4 – 2 5/8" x 3" rectangles (template E)

From the dark fabric, cut

- 2 – 3 7/8 squares, cut each square once on the diagonal making four triangles (or cut four triangles using template B)

For each Square Diamond block, you will need to make four half-square triangles. To do so, draw a diagonal line from corner to corner on the reverse side of the two 3 3/8" background squares. Place each light square atop a medium light square with right sides facing and sew 1/4" on both sides of the line. Using your rotary cutter and ruler, cut along the line. Open each half-square triangle unit and press toward the darker fabric.

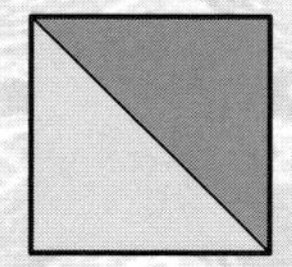

Sew a half-square triangle to the long sides of an E rectangle. The lightest part of the half-square triangles should be toward the center. Make two strips like this.

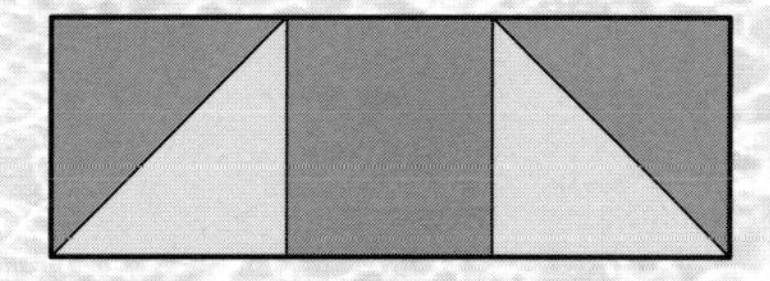

Then sew an E rectangle to opposite sides of the F square.

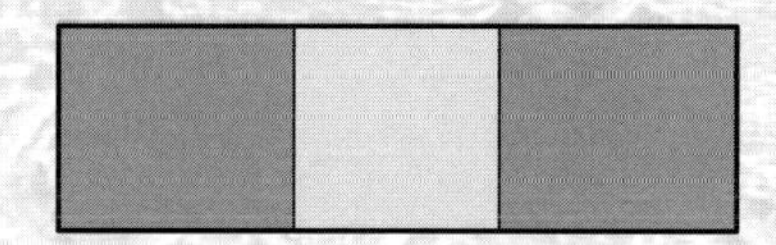

Sew the three rows together as shown to complete the center portion of the block.

Miter the corners of the C strips using template C as a guide. Sew a C strip to teach of the short sides of a B triangle. Avoid sewing into the seam allowance at the point but sew all the way to the end of the seams. Make four of the corner units.

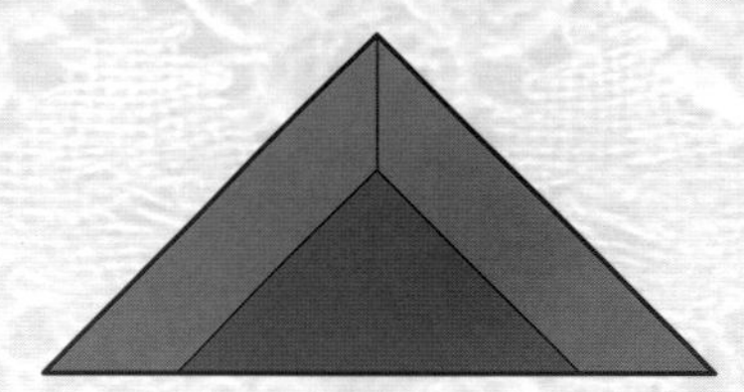

Turn the center unit on point and add the four corner units.

Miter the corners of the A strips using template A as a guide. Add the A strips to complete the block as shown.

A
C
D
B
D
E
F
B
E
F
D

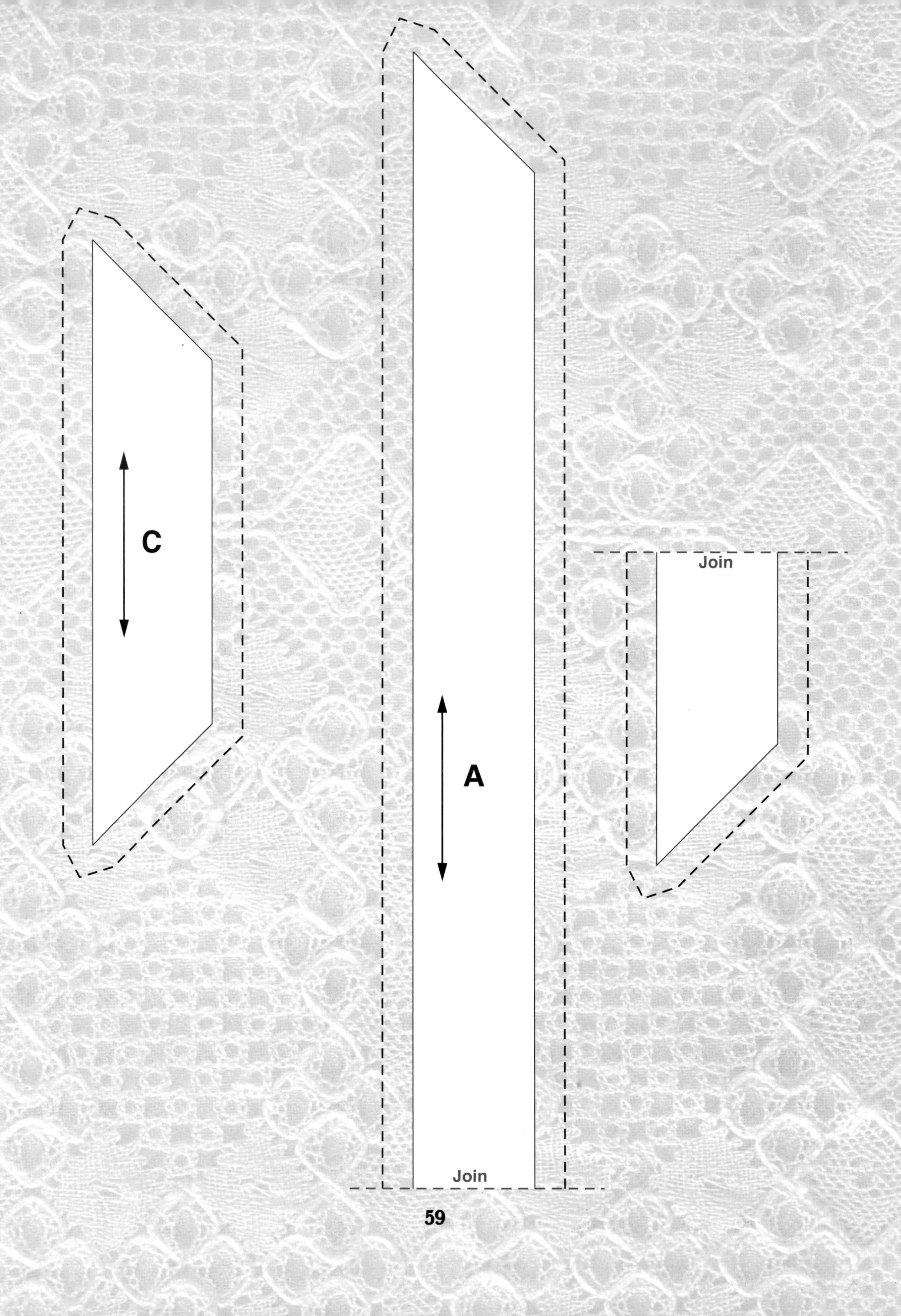
C
A
Join
Join

QUEEN'S JEWELS

Clara Diaz, Independence, Missouri, pieced and quilted her own version of *Diamonds Are . . .* using different fabrics and named it *Queen's Jewels*.

BERNIE & CLARA DIAZ

Bernie and Clara Diaz grew up in the small town of Eskridge, Kansas. Clara knew Bernie's younger sister and two brothers when she was in grade school but didn't actually meet him until she began her freshman year in high school. He was in his senior year when they began dating.

Clara, who was the eldest child in a family of six girls, was sure he was the right person for her. "He used to take my little sisters along when we went to the drive-in movies," she said. "He would let my sisters polish his toenails red and not get angry with them."

After two years of dating, the two married. There really was no proposal, just a lot of talk between them about how they would live and what they would do once they were married. Bernie's and Clara's mothers were the witnesses at their small wedding in the courthouse in Topeka, Kansas.

They have celebrated 48 1/2 years together. Clara and Bernie reared five children, one daughter and four sons, and now have grandchildren to cherish. One granddaughter is named after Clara and is well on her way to becoming a quilter like her grandmother.

They attribute the success of their marriage to their children, their parents, and their siblings.

They also think growing up in a small town and having similar experiences was a contributing factor. When asked if they would do it all over again, Bernie said, "Yes! Yes! Yes!"

Advice? They have this to offer, "Learn to talk to each other. Get to know and respect each other's families. Try to have some common interests but understand that you can each have your own interests that the other may not share. Discuss and come to an agreement ahead of time about life goals, children, discipline and how to handle money."

Clara, Bernie and daughter Micki.

Amethysts and Emeralds

AMETHYSTS AND EMERALDS

Made by Edie McGinnis, Brenda Butcher, Clara Diaz, Judy Hill, Judy Lovell, Margaret Falen, Karlene Cooper. Quilted by Nedra Forbes, Liberty, Missouri.

AMETHYSTS AND EMERALDS

12" Block

Quilt Size: Approximately 87" x 96"

The original amethyst pattern ran in *The Star* in 1931. I have altered the pattern to make it easier to piece. I divided the entire block into fourths. Now, instead of cutting one square for the center and insetting a large triangle between each point, you will be able to piece 1/4 of the block at a time. Since I don't care much for square quilts, I have added a 15" pillow tuck and appliquéd 6 four-pointed jewels across the top.

To make the quilt, you will need:

- 4 3/4 yards of dark purple (includes borders, pillow tuck and binding)
- 1 yard medium purple
- 1 3/4 yards of dark green
- 2 1/2 yards of lighter mottled green

Cutting instructions:

From the dark purple, cut 11 – 6 7/8" strips across the width of the fabric. Cut 144 triangles using template C. By inverting the triangle every other cut, you should be able to get 14 triangles from each strip. You will also need to cut 6" strips for three of the borders and one 15" strip for the pillow tuck. In order to get the length measurement of these cuts, you will need to measure the quilt top after the blocks are put together. I included enough fabric for you to be able to cut your borders and pillow tuck along the lengthwise grain.

From the medium purple fabric, cut 8—3 7/8" strips across the width of the fabric. Cut the strips into 3 7/8" squares. Each strip should yield 10 squares. Cut each of the squares from corner to corner on the diagonal, making half-square triangles. You need 144 triangles (template B).

From the dark green fabric, cut 15 – 3 5/8" strips across the width of the fabric. Cut the strips into 3 5/8" x 7 1/4" rectangles. Cut the rectangles for corner to corner on the diagonal (template A). Trim the points with a point trimmer or by cutting out template A. You will need 72 A pieces and 72 Ar pieces, so make sure your fabric is folded when you are cutting.

From the lighter, mottled green fabric, cut 15 – 3 5/8" strips across the width of the fabric. Cut the strips into 3 5/8" x 7 1/4" rectangles. Cut the rectangles from corner to corner on the diagonal (template A). Trim the points with a point trimmer or by cutting out template A. You will need 72 A pieces and 72 Ar pieces, so make sure your fabric is folded when you are cutting. You will also need to cut 2 1/2" strips for the framing border. You will have to measure your quilt to get the lengths needed.

For the appliquéd jewels, cut:

- 6 – 3 5/16" squares (template D) from the dark green fabric

- 24 triangles using template E from the mottled green fabric

To make the block:

Sew a dark green A and a dark green Ar triangle to the long sides of a large purple C triangle. Add a medium purple B triangle. This makes 1/4 of the block.

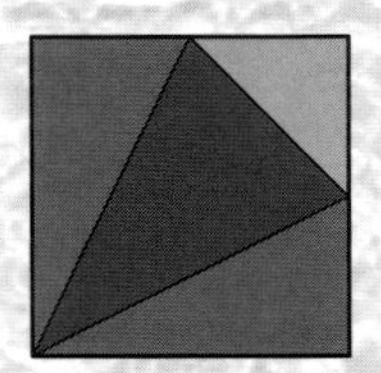

Sew a light mottled green A and a light mottled green Ar to the long sides of a large purple C triangle. Add a medium purple B triangle. This makes the second quarter of the block.

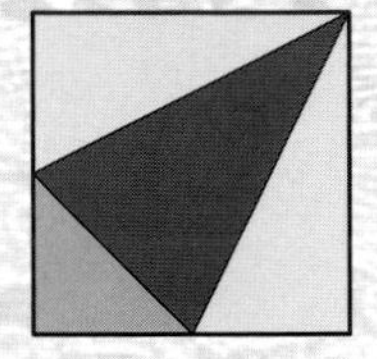

Now sew a dark green Ar triangle and a mottled green A triangle to opposite sides of a large purple C triangle. Add a medium purple B triangle. This makes the third quarter of the block.

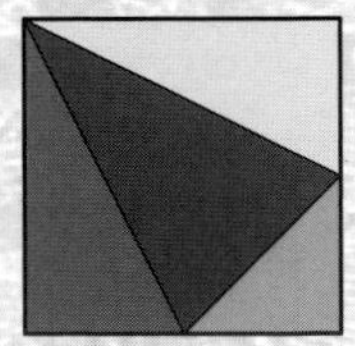

For the last quarter of the block, sew a dark green A triangle to one side of a large purple C triangle and a mottled green Ar triangle to the other side. Add a medium purple B triangle.

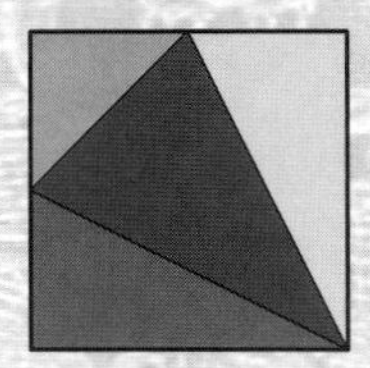

Sew the four quarters of the block together as shown.

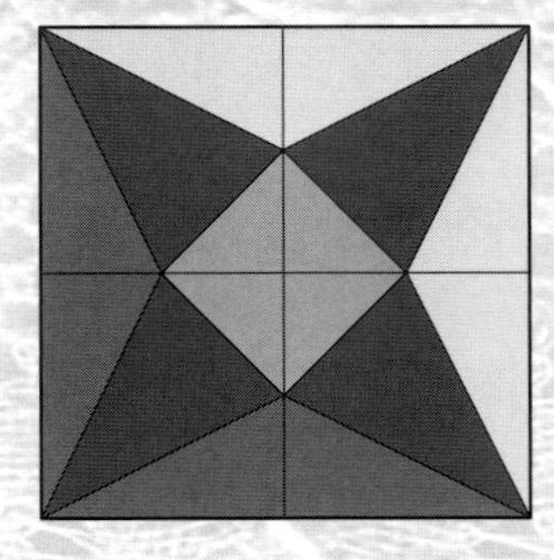

Make 36 blocks. Sew the blocks into 6 rows across and 6 rows down. We found it was far easier to keep track of color placement by sewing the blocks into sections of four as shown. When you sew the four blocks together, the mottled green is always toward the inside of the section and the dark green is always toward the outside of the section.

After the blocks are sewn together, measure the quilt through the center from top to bottom. Sew enough 2 1/2" mottled green strips together to equal the length. Sew a strip to each side of the quilt. Now measure the quilt top through the middle from side to side and sew enough 2 1/2" mottled green strips together to equal that measurement. Sew the strips to the top and bottom of the quilt.

Again, measure the quilt through the center from top to bottom. Cut 2 – 6" strips to equal that measurement and sew a strip to each side of the quilt. Measure the quilt through the center and cut 1 - 6" strip and 1 – 15" strip that length. Sew the 6" strip to the bottom of the quilt and the 15" strip to the top.

Make 6 emeralds to appliqué across the top of the pillow tuck.

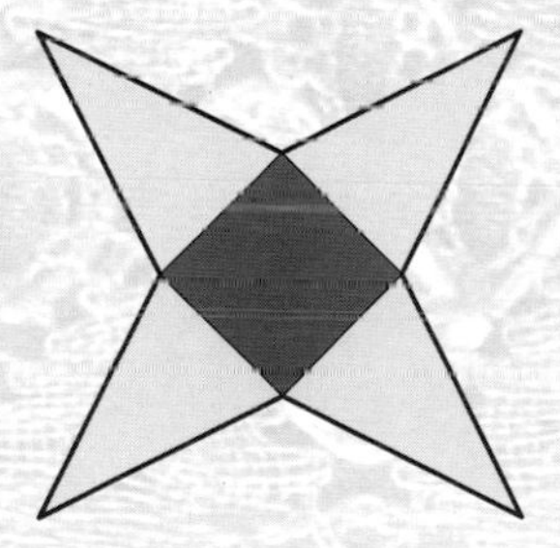

Sew four E pieces to each D square as shown. Appliqué each emerald in place in a whimsical fashion. Refer to the photo for placement.

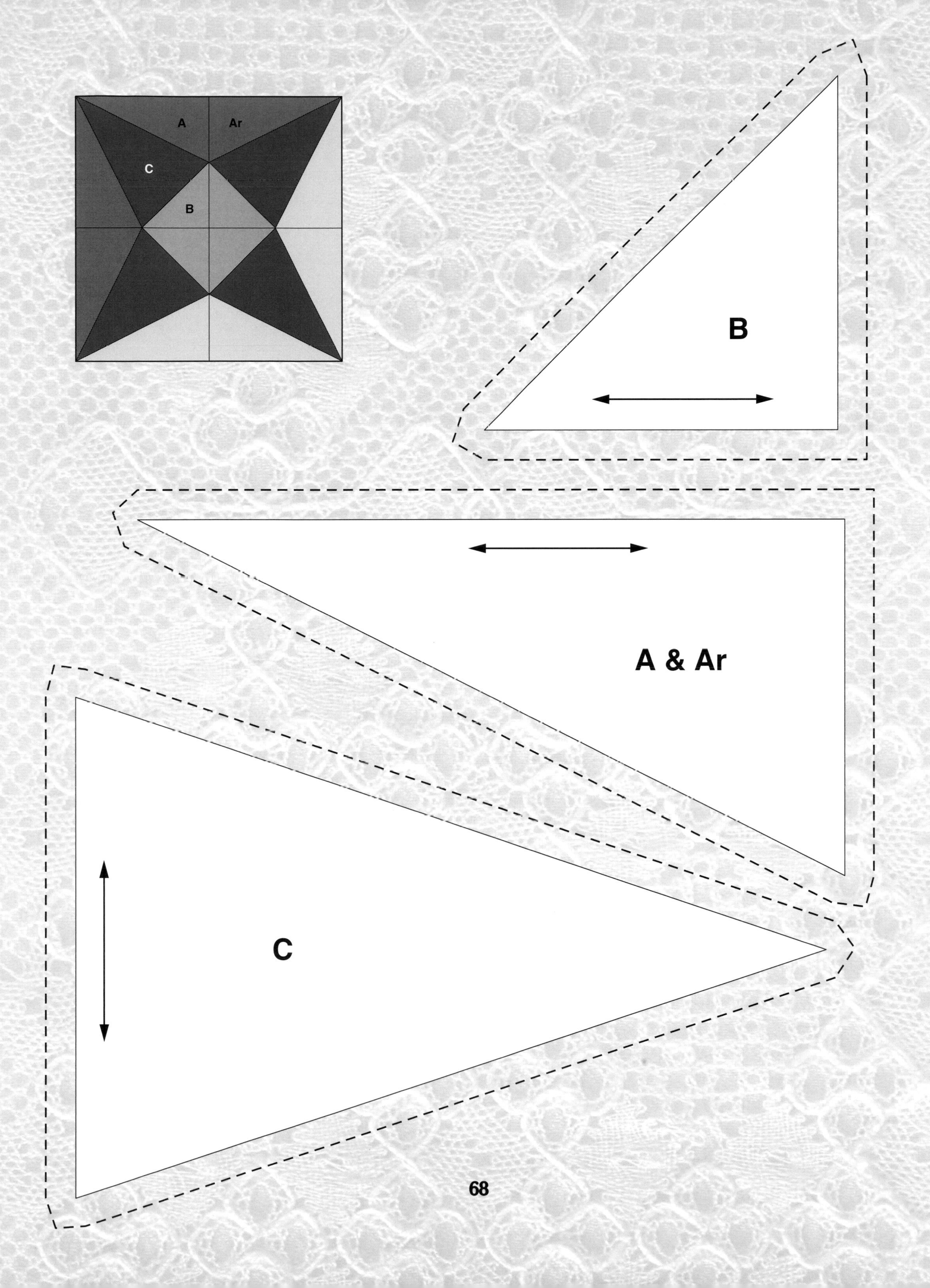
A
Ar
C
B
B
A & Ar
C

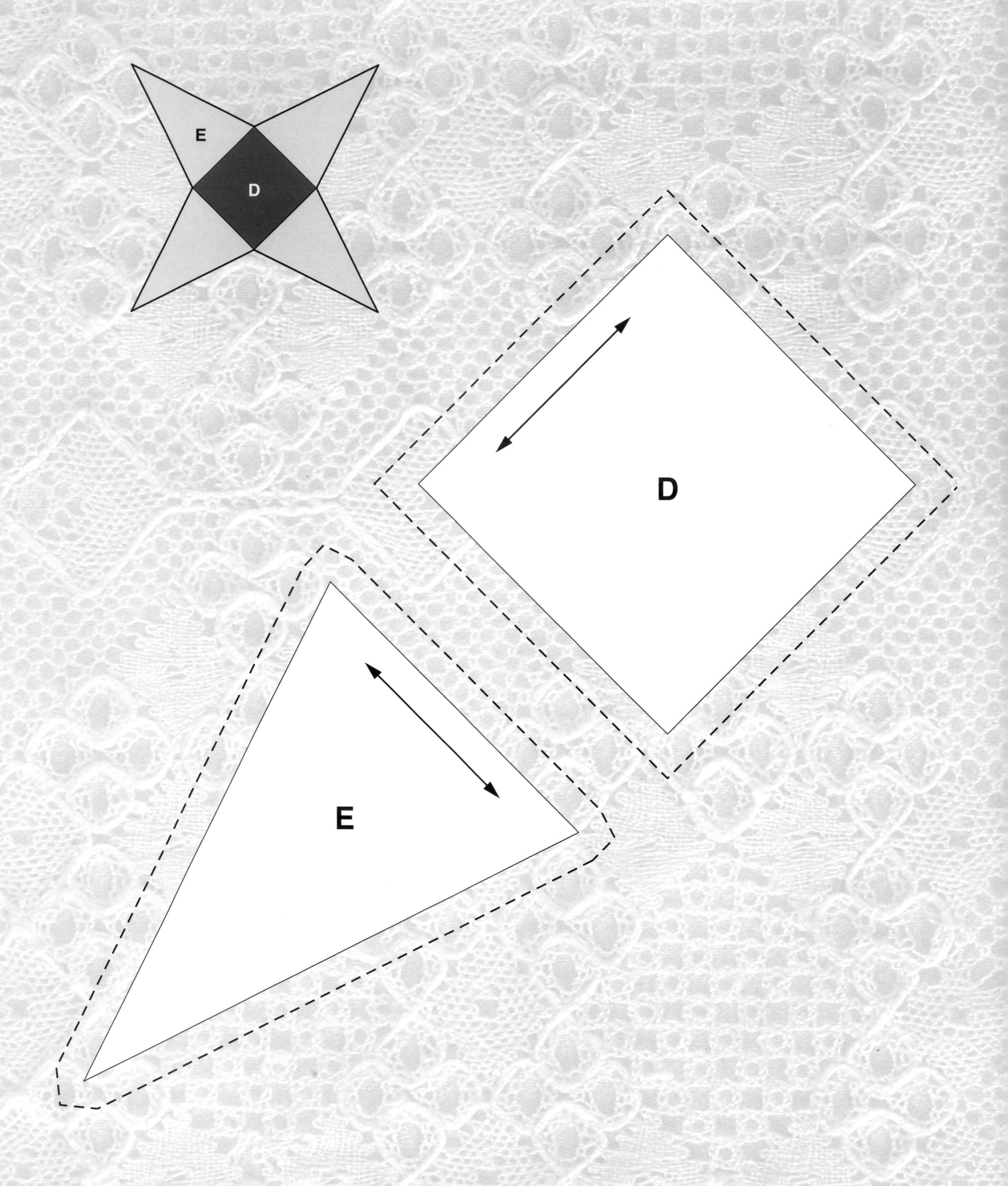
E
D
D
E

This is four blocks put together.

DAVE AND RUBY DOWNING

Dave and Ruby Downing met in the crystal laboratory in the Research and Development Company at 15th and McGee in Kansas City, Missouri, where Ruby worked making radio crystals. Dave was the foreman for the construction company that had been contracted to remodel the building in which Ruby worked.

Ruby caught Dave's eye and he asked her to go out to dinner with him. They went to Weisses' Restaurant in Kansas City for a roast duckling dinner. "Oh, it was so good and I was so full!" Ruby said. "When he took me home, I really wanted to get that snug dress off and my comfy, old housecoat on, but I decided to suffer, as it didn't seem appropriate to take off my dress on a first date."

Ruby knew Dave was a hard worker. He was also about her age and she took a shine to the way he looked. He seemed to be her kind of guy. They dated for two years before they married. Going on picnics was one of their favorite pastimes They would bundle the children, Dave's three and Ruby's two, into the car and spend the day at Swope Park.

The two had a small, informal wedding at a Congregational Church in Kansas City. Ruby's mother and stepfather were the witnesses. She made her dress and he bought a new suit for the occasion. Ruby's mother brought flowers from her garden for the tiny reception at Ruby's apartment.

Their marriage has lasted for 49 years. Both say they would do it all over again; Dave just wouldn't wait as long.

When asked why their marriage has survived, Ruby said, "We agree on the important things: finances, mutual fidelity and trust. We allow each other space. He likes my cooking, although he can and has taken over the management of the house when illness has put me down. We both enjoy reading. We have similar taste in music.

"If we have a disagreement, we sort of let it go – it usually just works itself out. We don't harp on each other's faults; we don't bitch or scream at each other."

They enjoy each other's company too. "I told someone the other day that I had to get on home. When she asked why, I said, 'Cause he's there.' I thought about that for a bit and realized that anytime Dave and I are separated, no matter the amount of time, I think only of getting home – to Dave. And he feels the same – to get home to Ruby. So, I guess it'll last."

Their advice to couples getting married today? The Downings had this to offer:

"Forget the big wedding and expensive honeymoon. Instead, have a little wedding and a weekend trip to a nice, quiet motel with room service. Forget buying that big house with its huge debt and back-breaking housework. Forget the house full of new furniture, the wall-size TV, the two new cars and the shopping sprees, and especially, cut up the credit cards!!"

Gold and Rubies

GOLD AND RUBIES

Made by Peggy McFeeters, Morton, Illinois.

Quilted by Nedra Forbes, Liberty, Missouri.

GOLD AND RUBIES

15" Block

Quilt Size: 81" x 96"

This quilt is made by combining two *Kansas City Star* patterns, Bright Jewel and Single Wedding Ring. It would make a perfect gift for a couple celebrating their 40th (Ruby) wedding anniversary.

Fabric Requirements:

- Gold – 4 yards Red – 6 yards (includes border and binding)

For a large quilt you will need to make 30 blocks, 15 Bright Jewel Blocks and 15 Single Wedding Ring Blocks. Both patterns are made using only squares and half-square triangles and the size of the pieces are the same.

From the red fabric, cut:

- 21 – 3 1/2" strips
  Set 9 strips aside for the borders and cut the remaining 12 strips into 3 1/2" squares. You need 135 squares.

- 24 – 3 7/8" strips. Cut the strips into 3 7/8" squares. You need 240 squares.

From the gold fabric, cut:

- 12 – 3 1/2" strips. Cut the strips into 3 1/2" squares. You need 135 squares.

- 24 – 3 7/8" strips. Cut the strips into 3 7/8" squares. You need 240 squares.

Place a gold 3 7/8" square atop a red 3 7/8" square. Draw a 45 degree line from corner to corner on the gold square. Sew 1/4" on each side of the line. Cut on the line. Open each half-square triangle and press. You will need to make 480 of these units for the quilt.

Using the squares and half-square triangles, make 15 Bright Jewel blocks by following diagram A and 15 Single Wedding Ring blocks by following diagram B.

Diagram A

Diagram B

Set the blocks together in 6 horizontal rows. Each row has five blocks. Rows 1, 3 and 5 begin and end with a Bright Jewel block. Rows 2, 4 and 6 begin and end with a Single Wedding Ring block.

For the border, sew two red strips together for the top and bottom. Sew 2 1/2 strips together for each side border. Sew the borders to the top and bottom of the quilt, then add a border to the left and right sides. Layer the top, backing and batting and quilt. Bind the quilt to finish it.

BRIGHT JEWEL

SINGLE WEDDING RING

A
B

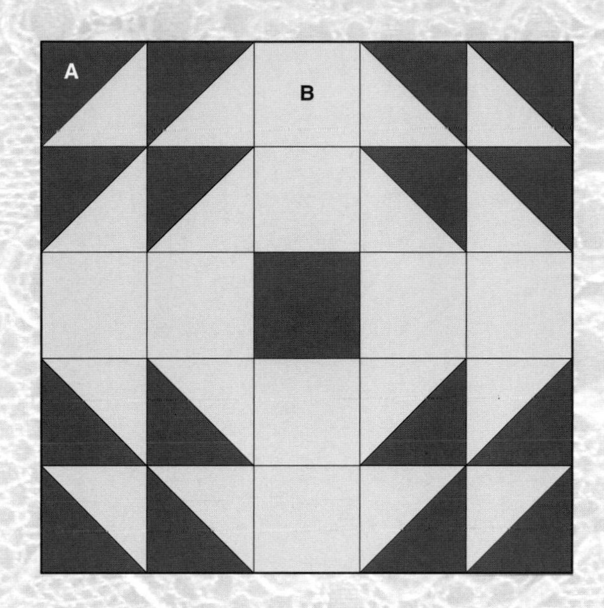
A
B

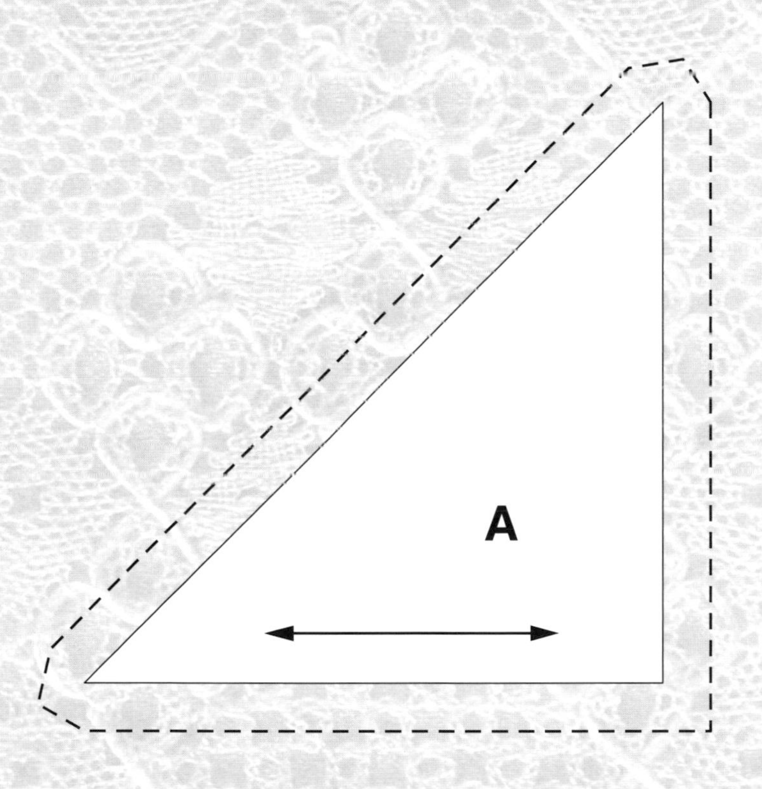
A

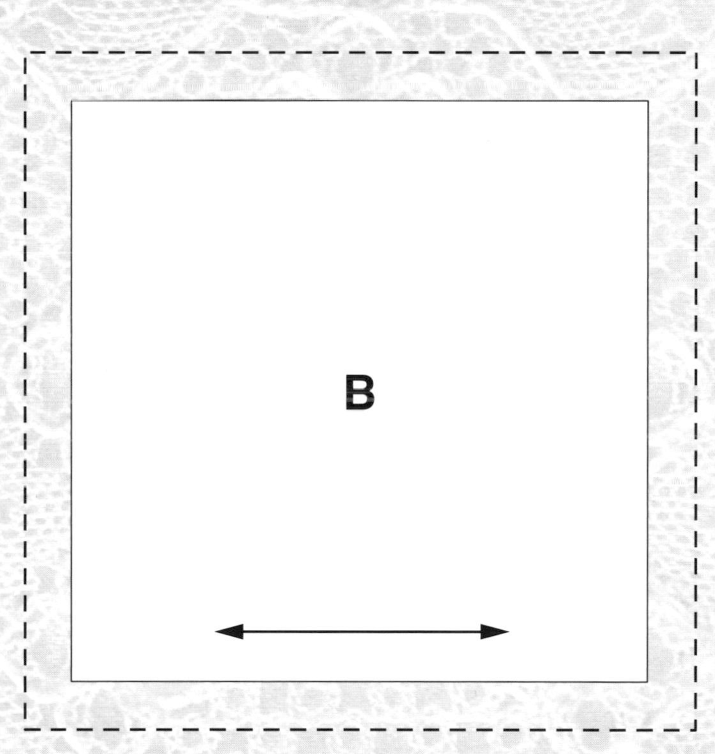
B

SHARI AND HOWARD MCMILLAN

The McMillans celebrated their 48th wedding anniversary in March of 2005. They have two children, Kevin, a horticulturist, and Ken, a veterinarian. Both are married.

They first met at a DeMolay and Job's Daughters Valentine's Day dance where Howard asked Shari to dance with him. That in itself was enough to make her heart do flip-flops. She remembers being a skinny, gawky kid that didn't know how to dance. He remembers her being the cutest girl at the dance. They began dating and, like teenagers will, fell for each other.

A few years later, the couple decided to elope. Shari was 16 and Howard was 19. They left in Howard's Buick and drove to Mississippi, where they found that the minister of the Methodist church in Victoria, Mississippi, wouldn't marry them without permission from one of Shari's parents. They reached into their reservoir of courage and made the call, and after all the parental wailing was done, permission was granted.

There weren't too many people who thought the marriage would last. Howard thinks they were successful for many reasons. He says, "You need to be good friends first. Your spouse needs to be the most important person in your life. You won't always agree on everything but you shouldn't have angry discussions in the presence of your children. Most importantly, always be in agreement where your children are concerned. Sometimes this means a private, calm discussion to reach a consensus." "Besides," Shari added with a grin, "it's easier to stay together than start all over again."

Howard also thinks it is important to have interests in common. Both of them hold Scouting's highest council award, both love wild flowers, are co-winners of the Rotary Club's Service to Youth award, and enjoy the same kind of vacations.

Shari and Howard offer this advice to people considering getting married. She says, "Be good friends first and stay friends. Develop good communication skills." Howard adds, "Don't be in a hurry. Get to know each other well. You need to be very good friends first."

Square and Diamonds

SQUARE AND DIAMONDS

Made by Shari McMillan, Marquette Heights, Illinois.

Quilted by Nedra Forbes, Liberty, Missouri.

SQUARE AND DIAMONDS

12" Block

Quilt Size: 70" x 82"

Fabric needed:

- Light – 3 yards (includes fabric for 3" finished border)
- Medium – 2 1/2 yards (includes fabric for binding)
- Dark – 3 1/4 yards (includes 2" finished inner border)

From the medium fabric, cut:

- 3 strips 3 1/2" deep across the width of the fabric. Recut the strips into 3 1/2" squares or use template D. You need 30 squares and each strip should yield 12 squares.

- 15 strips 2 1/2" deep across the width of the fabric. Recut the strips into diamonds using template C. You need to cut 120 diamonds. Each strip should yield 8.

From the light fabric, cut:

- 20 strips 3 1/2" deep across the width of the fabric. Recut the strips into trapezoids using template B. Each strip should yield 6 pieces and you need a total of 120.

- 9 strips 3 1/2" deep across the width of the fabric. Set these strips aside for the framing border.

From the dark fabric, cut:

- 40 strips 2" deep across the width of the fabric. Recut each strip into trapezoids using template A. Each strip should yield 3 pieces and you will need a total of 120.

- 8 strips, 2 1/2" deep across the width of the fabric for the inner border

To make each block:

Sew piece A to piece B. Make four of these units.

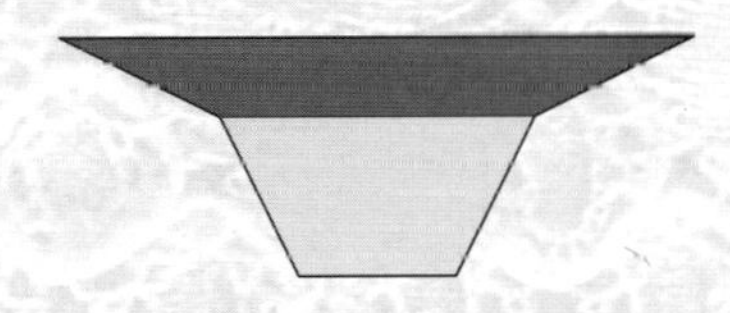

Sew a C diamond to each side of two of the AB units. Begin at the point of the diamond that intersects the seam between piece A and piece B. Sew to one end of the diamond point. Lift the pressure foot of your sewing machine, go back to the diamond point where you began and sew to the other end of the diamond point.

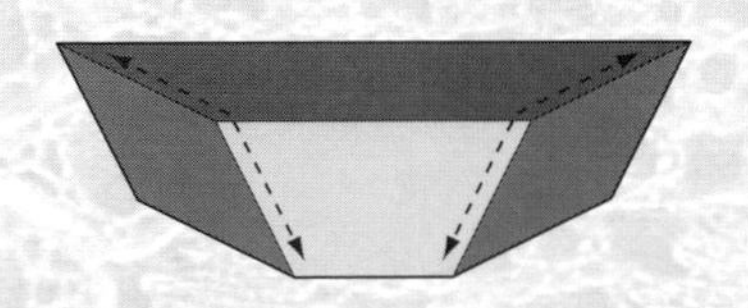

Sew the two remaining AB units to opposite sides of the D square.

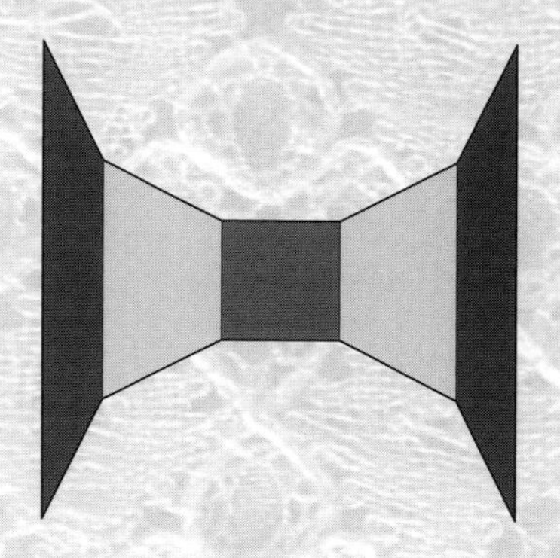

Add an AB unit that has the diamonds sewn on to the center square. Sew the seam to the square first. Then stitch the remaining seams together. Begin with the point of the diamond that intersects the seam line between piece A and piece B. Sew toward the center of the block. Lift your pressure foot, go back to the diamond point and finish the seam by sewing to the outer part of the block.

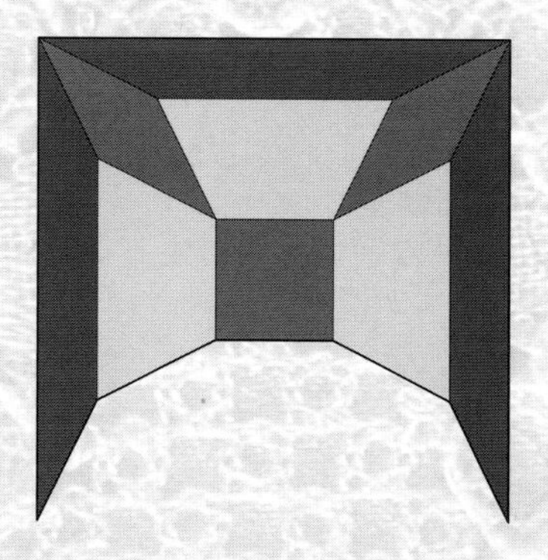

Add the remaining AB unit with the diamonds to complete the block. Sew to the block in the same manner as above.

Sew the blocks together. The example shows a setting of 5 blocks across and 6 blocks down. Add a 2 inch finished framing border using the dark 2 1/2" fabric strips. Add a second border using the light 3 1/2" light fabric strips. The border should be 3" finished.

Layer the quilt with batting and backing and quilt.

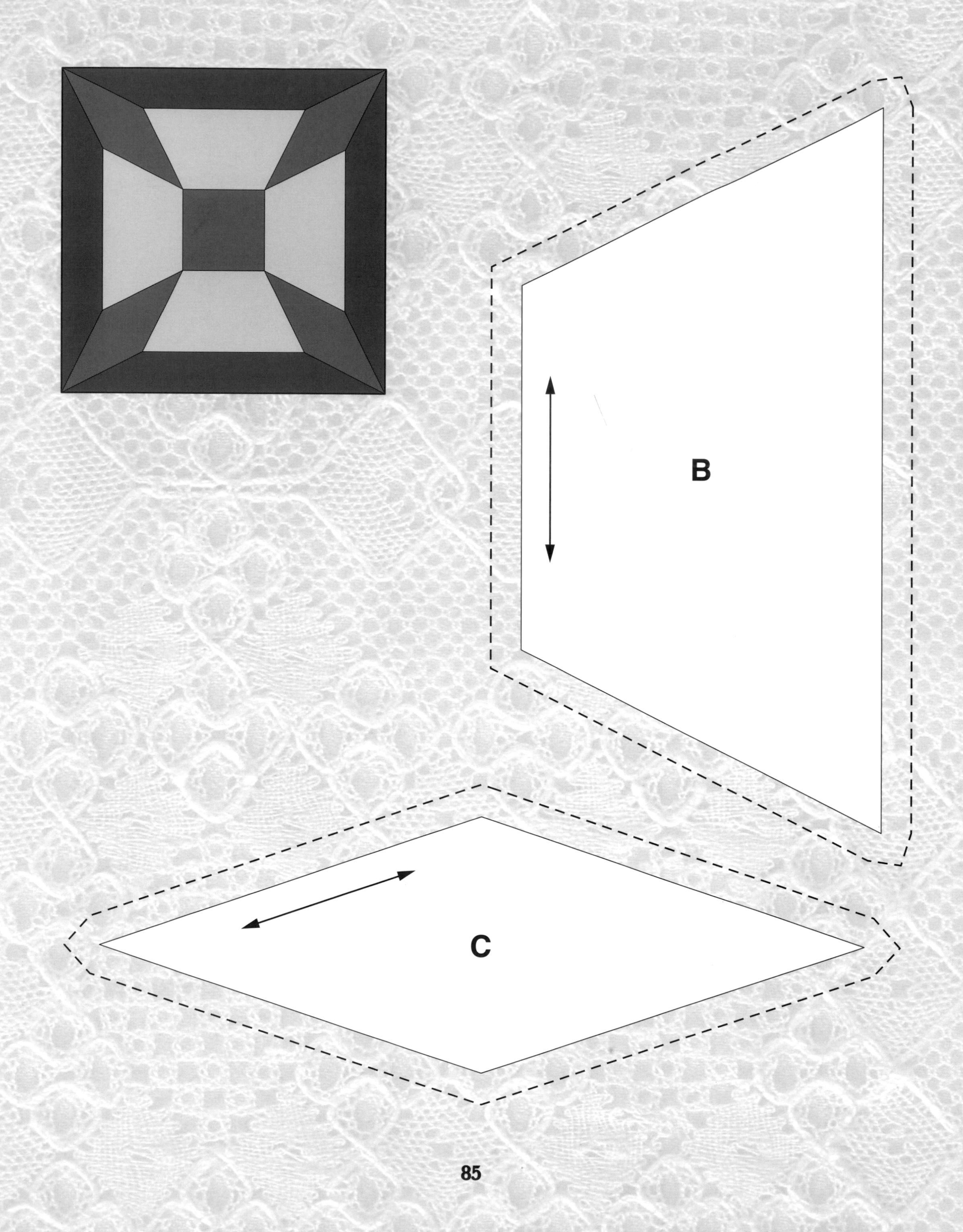
B
C

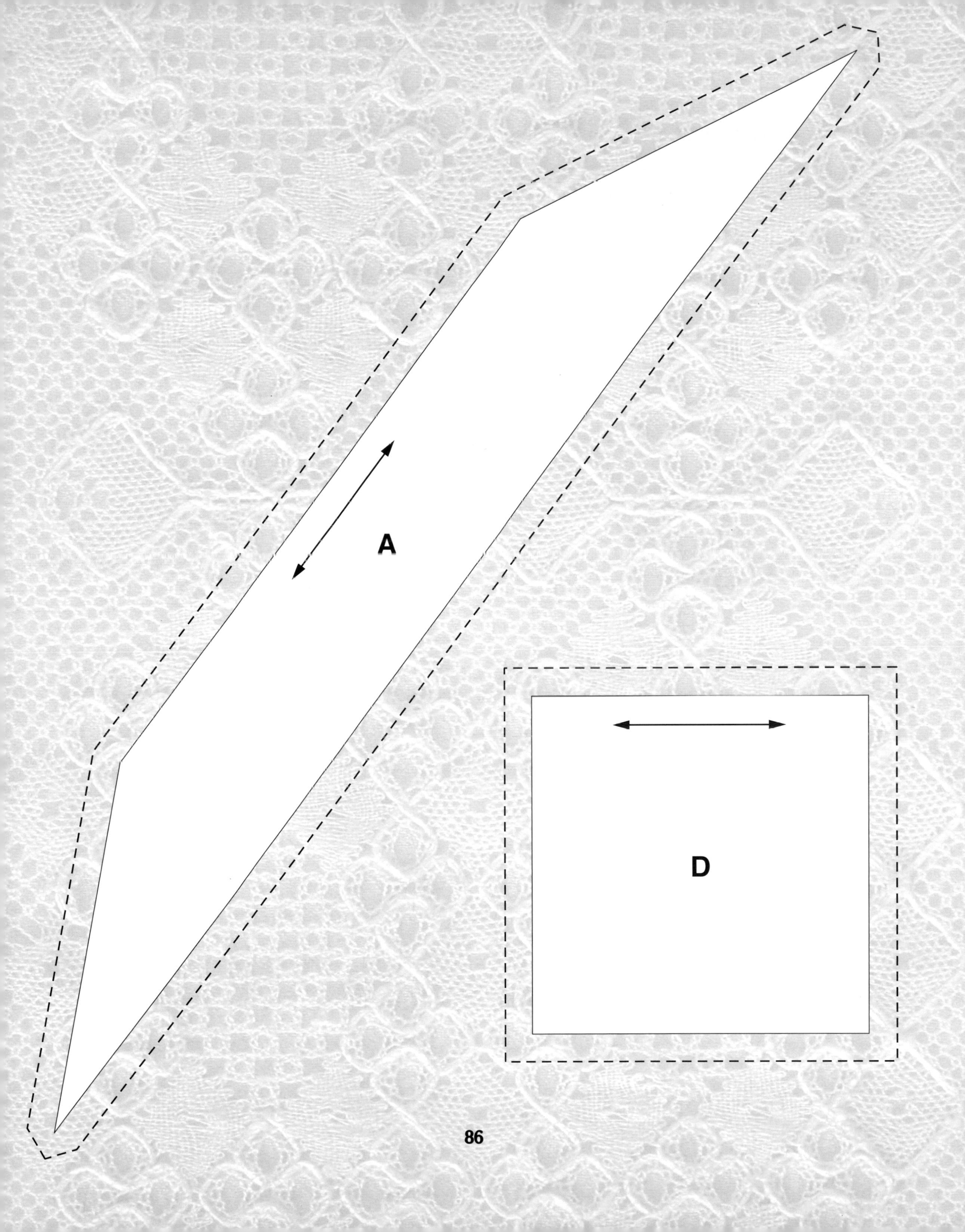
A
D

CORKY AND PEGGY HUTINETT

Corky (Francis) and Peggy Hutinett celebrated their 48th wedding anniversary on June 15, 2005. They were blessed with three children: Steve, Jennifer and Paul. They now have four granddaughters.

Peggy had just graduated with a degree in journalism from the University of Missouri at Columbia, Missouri, when she found a job with *The Raytown News* in Raytown, Missouri, writing stories and calling on advertisers every week. Corky had served for four years in the U.S. Navy in Korea. When he was discharged, he too found a job with *The Raytown News* running a press and hand-setting type.

Peggy played a game of Tom Sawyer on Corky on their first date. She invited him to come to her house to help paint the walls in the new addition her parents had built onto their house. In exchange, she offered him a home cooked meal. Corky says she has kept him busy ever since.

After dating off and on for three years, Corky finally popped the question. Rather than have a large, elaborate wedding, the two opted to buy a house in preparation for their life together. They were married in a small ceremony at Raytown Christian Church. Peggy's cousin, Doris, served as her matron of honor and Corky's brother was his best man. About thirty of their friends attended and, after the ceremony, went to the reception held at Peggy's parents' home. Peggy's mom and grandma baked the wedding cake.

When asked how Peggy knew Corky was the one person for her, she said, "I saw in him a gentleness, a wholesomeness, a caring for all things good. On that foundation, love could only flourish."

When asked the same question, Corky said, "When I held her hand, I could feel the transition of our spirits – one into the other."

Both say they have no regrets and would do it again, "in a New York minute."

I asked them why they thought in this day and age when so many marriages fail, they were still together. Corky replied, "Compatibility, commitment and companionship." Peggy's answer was, "For 48 years, I have prefaced each decision with 'How will Corky feel about this?' I think not 'me' but 'us.'"

They have these words of advice to offer to couples getting married today. "Have only one credit card and use it for emergencies – not necessities like groceries or unessentials like impulse items. Be fully committed to the marriage and don't live together first."

Paper Piecing

PAPER PIECING INSTRUCTIONS

I have redrafted some of these patterns so they can be paper pieced. Paper piecing can often simplify a difficult block, making it easier and quicker to piece.

1. To paper piece a block, cut your fabric about 1/2" larger than the piece needed all the way around.

2. Use a glue stick to adhere piece number 1 to the paper pattern. Hold the paper pattern with the fabric on it up to a light source to make sure the entire area is covered with fabric.

3. Place a postcard or index card along line number 1 and fold the paper back over the card.

4. Butt an Add-A-Quarter ruler up against the paper fold and trim the edge of piece number 1.

5. Place the next fabric in position number 2.

6. Again, check to see if the fabric covers the space allotted. If the fabric covers the space, flip the piece back over the first fabric with right sides facing.

7. Sew along the line between piece number 1 and piece number 2.

8. Open the piece and add piece number three as indicated on the pattern and trim.

9. Continue on in this manner until each unit is complete.

10. Sew all the units together and complete the block.

11. Trim as you go using your Add-A-Quarter ruler.

12. Sew all your blocks together before you tear off the paper.

You may photocopy the paper piecing patterns on the following pages for your own private use: 29, 30, 94, 95, 100, 101, 108, 109, 114, 115, 122, and 123.

Star Sapphire

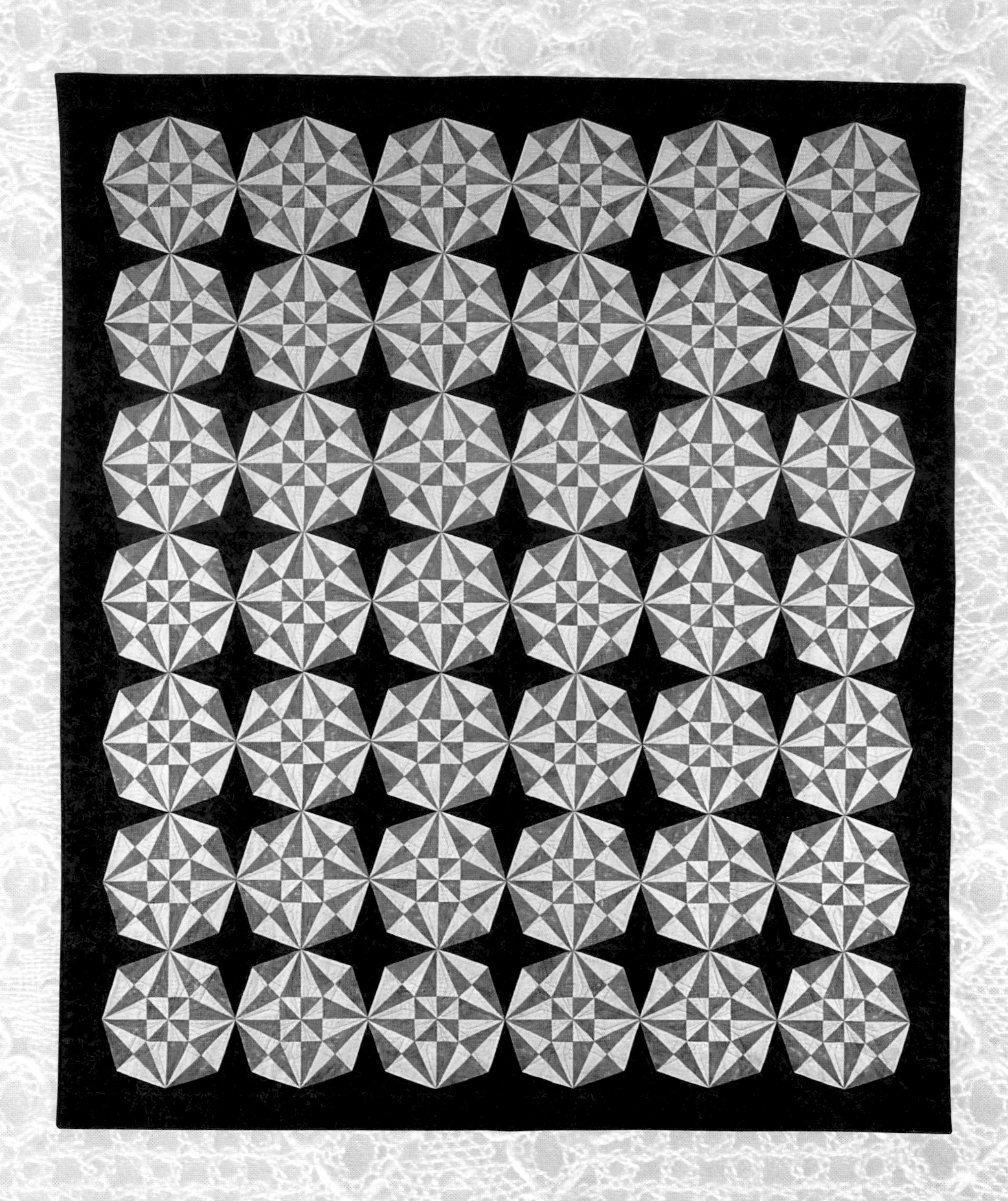

STAR SAPPHIRE

Made by Sue McNamara, Peoria, Illinois.

Quilted by Nedra Forbes, Liberty, Missouri.

STAR SAPPHIRE VARIATION

78" x 90"

This pattern was printed in *The Star* in 1936 with many of the pieces curved. I straightened the curves and changed it into a paper pieced pattern to make it easier to piece. The pattern still retains the look of jewel facets and also keeps the wonderful secondary pattern.

Fabric needed:

- 5 yards of dark blue (includes enough fabric for the borders and the binding)
- 4 yards of medium blue
- 4 yards of light blue

Follow the paper piecing instructions on page 89. Make 42 blocks.

Unit A

- Fabric A – Dark Blue – will always go in position No. 1
- Fabric B – Medium Blue – will always go in positions No. 2 and No. 4
- Fabric C – Light Blue – will always go in positions No. 3 and No. 5

Unit B

- Fabric A – Dark Blue – will always go in position No. 1
- Fabric B – Medium Blue – will always go in positions No. 3 and No. 5
- Fabric C – Light Blue – will always go in positions No. 2 and No. 4

Each block is made using four A Units and four B Units. After sewing the fabric onto the paper, sew Unit A to Unit B along the diagonal edge. This makes one fourth of the block. You will need to make 42 blocks for the quilt.

After piecing the blocks, sew them into rows. You will need to make seven rows with each row containing six blocks. Wait until you have all the blocks sewn together to tear off the paper.

Cut 9 - 3" strips across the width of the fabric. Measure the quilt through the center from top to bottom. Sew enough strips together end to end to equal the length of the quilt. Sew the strips to the sides of the quilt. Measure the quilt through the center from side to side. Sew enough strips together to equal this measurement. Sew the strips to the top and bottom of the quilt.

Layer the backing, batting and top. Quilt and bind.

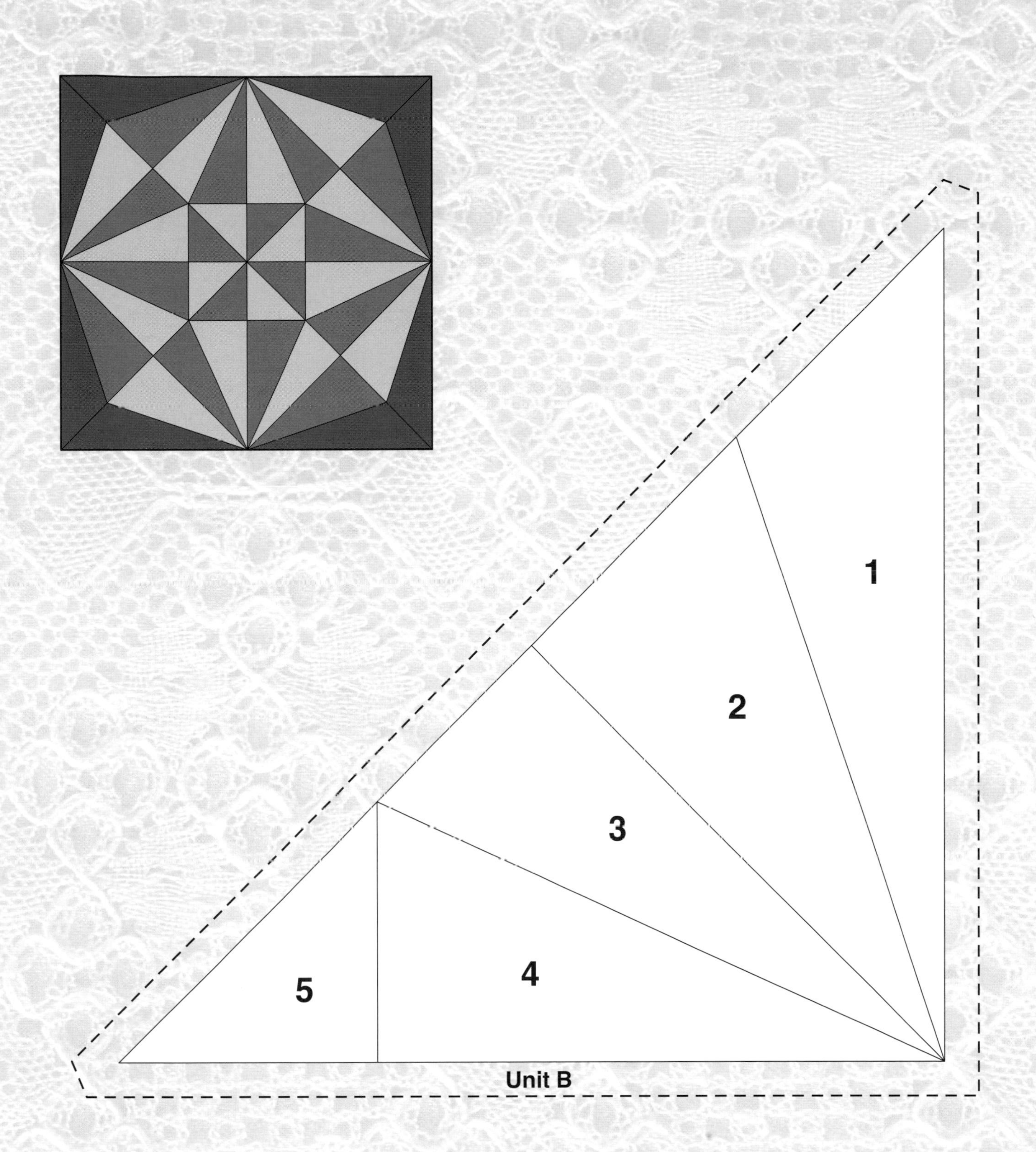
1
2
3
4
5
Unit B

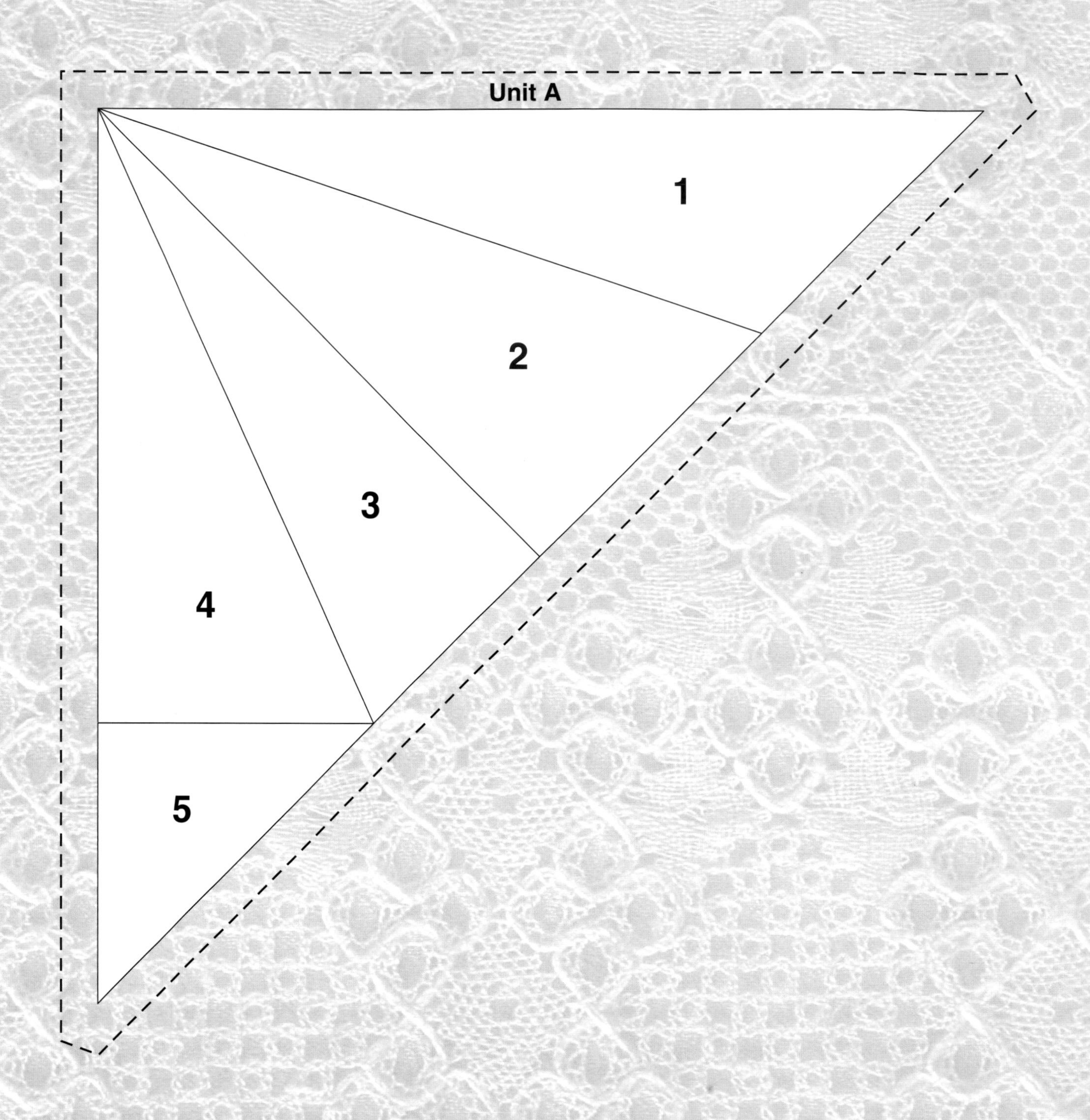
Unit A
1
2
3
4
5

Coverlet in Jewel Tones

COVERLET IN JEWEL TONES

Made by Dee Clevenger and Brenda Butcher, Independence, Missouri.
Quilted by Nedra Forbes, Liberty, Missouri.

COVERLET IN JEWEL TONES

Quilt Size: Approximately 81" x 93"

Fabric Needed:

- A - 5 yards dark purple - (includes small framing border)
- B - 2 1/2 yards teal
- C - 1 2/3 yards dark teal with spots
- D - 2 yards light purple
- E - 4 yards floral teal (includes outer border and binding)
- F - 1 2/3 yards striped teal

The fabric is sewn to the paper in the order printed on the pattern.

To make Unit A, sew:

- Fabric B in positions 1 and 5
- Fabric A in position 4
- Fabric C in position 2
- Fabric E in position 3

To make Unit B, sew:

- Fabric B in positions 1 and 5
- Fabric A in position 4
- Fabric F in position 2
- Fabric D in position 3

Sew the two units together along the long edge of the triangle. This makes one quarter of the block. Make three more quarters. Sew the four together to make one block. You will need to make 42 blocks for the quilt.

Sew the blocks together in rows using 6 blocks across and 7 down.

After all the blocks are sewn together, tear off the paper and then add the borders.

To make the inner framing border, cut 8 - 1 1/2" strips across the width of the dark purple fabric. Measure the quilt through the center horizontally and vertically. Write the numbers down. Sew enough strips together to equal the measurement through the center of the quilt. Make the strips for all four sides of the quilt. If you are mitering the corners, be sure to leave enough fabric for that purpose.

The outer border is made using the floral teal. Cut the strips 4" wide. You will need to cut 9 strips across the width of the fabric. Follow the directions in the above paragraph. After making the borders, sew them to the quilt. Miter the borders if you choose.

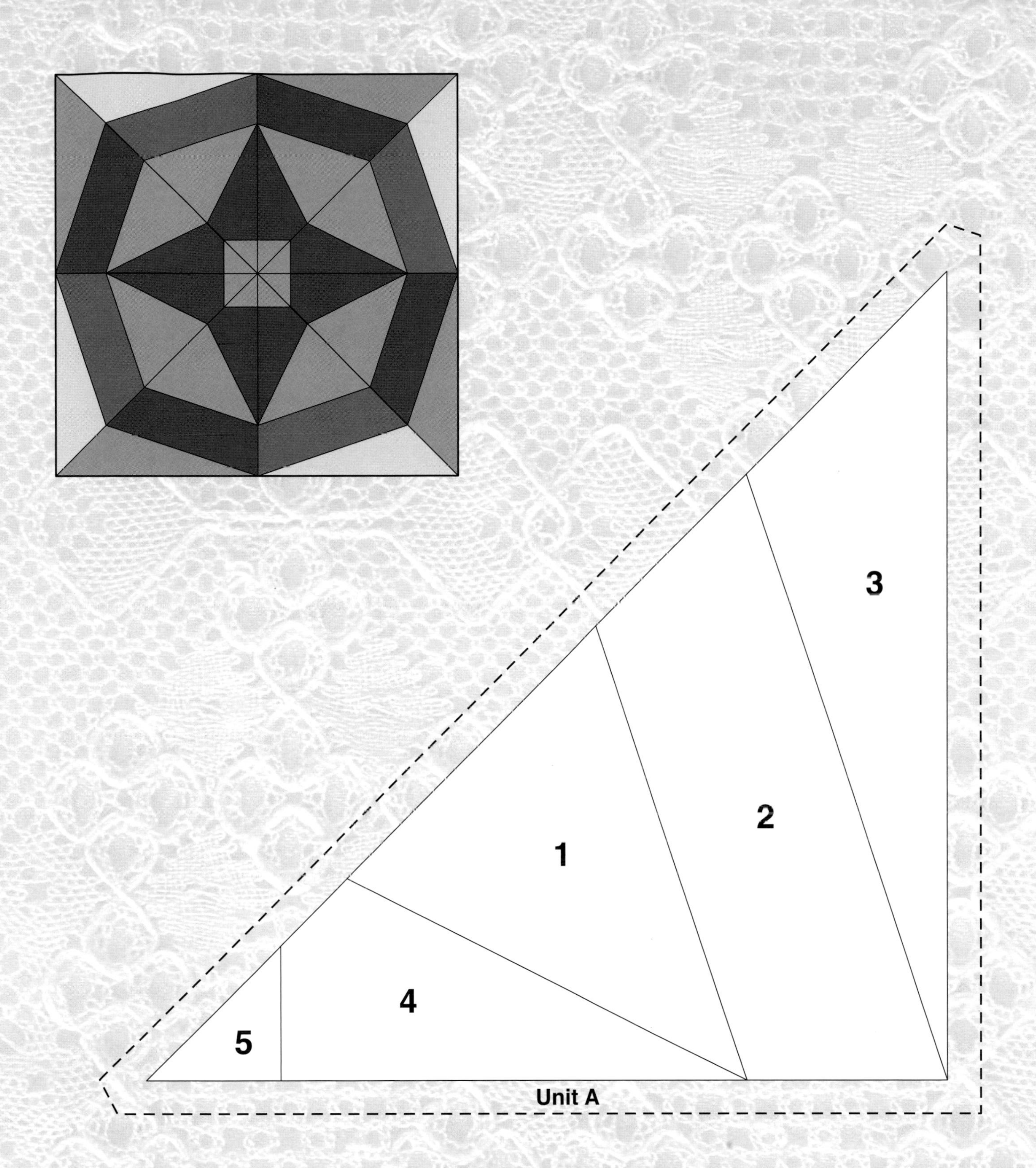
3
2
1
4
5
Unit A

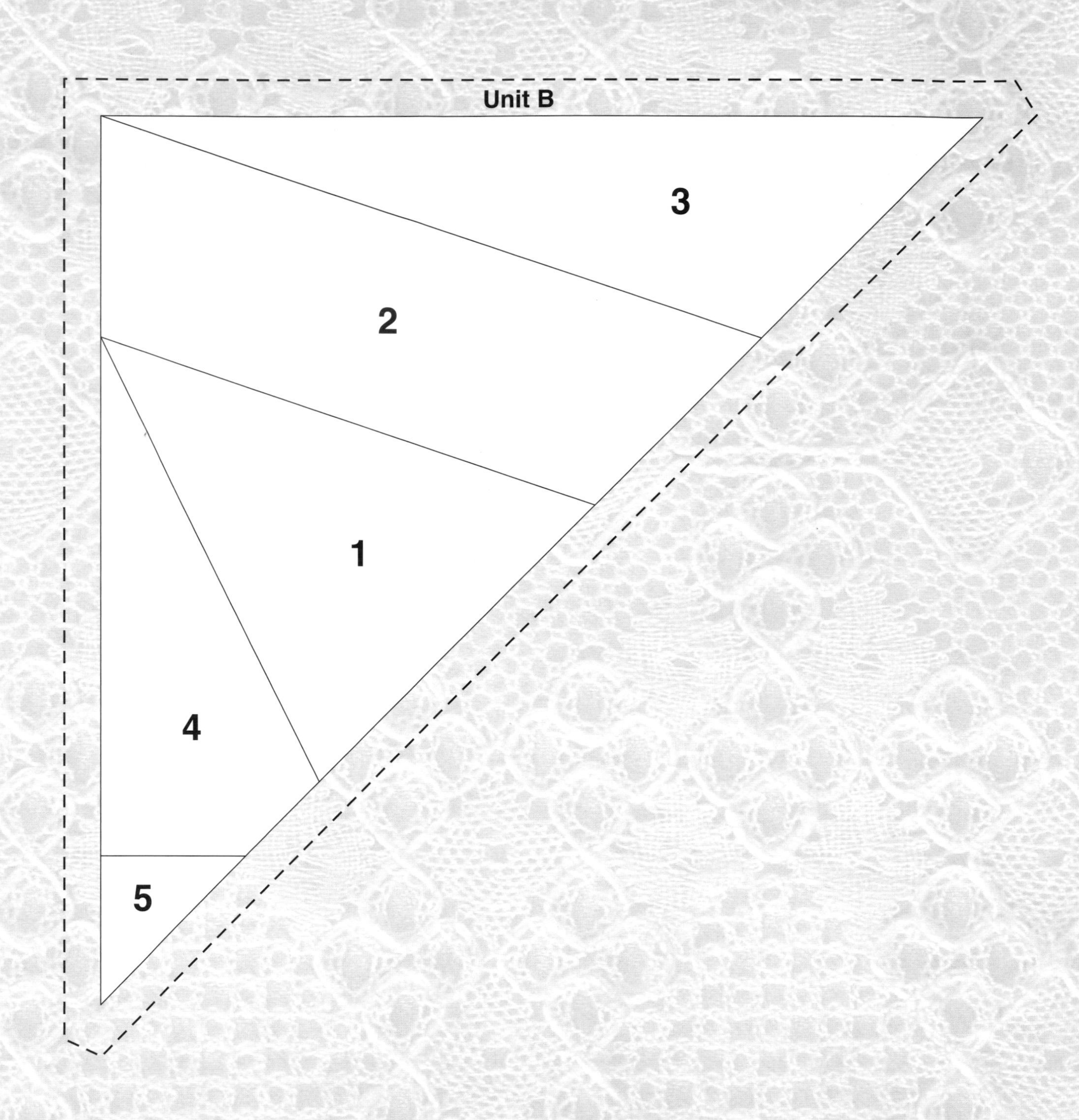
Unit B
3
2
1
4
5

KARLENE AND BOB COOPER

Karlene and Bob Cooper will celebrate 50 years together September 18, 2005. They have one son, Rob, who lives in Vietnam. Two and a half years ago, Rob and his wife gave Karlene and Bob their first grandchild, a boy named Hank.

Bob and Karlene met in Cherryvale, Kansas, where she had grown up. She was just beginning her senior year at Central High School in Kansas City, Missouri. Karlene had gone to Cherryvale to visit with a friend she had been close to since she was in the seventh grade. Her friend decided Karlene needed a date and set her up with Bob. The two couples went to the drive-in theater in Coffeyville, Kansas.

Bob asked her to go out with him again the following evening. They went to the stock car races without their friends. On that second date, Bob asked Karlene to marry him. "I wasn't ready to get married. I still had to finish my senior year in school."

The following May, Karlene went back to Cherryvale to her friend's graduation and ran into Bob. As the two were chatting, Bob told Karlene he had a date that night with a girl from Independence, Kansas. On his way out of town, Bob drove by the house where Karlene was staying and honked the horn. "Mad! I was so mad at him!" Karlene said. Then she laughed and said, "But we made up the following day."

After Bob joined the Navy, they wrote to each other. When he got out of boot camp, he proposed again. This time he got the answer he was looking for. They set the wedding date for August 14, 1955. Bob's emergency appendectomy made a change of plans mandatory. The two were finally married on September 18, 1955.

They had the wedding Karlene dreamed of. About seventy-five of their friends and family attended. It was held in the Methodist Church of Cherryvale, Kansas. Karlene was the fourth generation of her family to attend that church.

After the wedding the couple moved to Jacksonville, Florida, where Bob was stationed. Even though they sometimes didn't know where their next meal was coming from, they were happy. Karlene said, "Those three years living in Jacksonville really made us depend on each other.

Asked if they would marry one another again if they had it to do over, Bob replied, "Oh yes, for sure." Karlene agrees and says, "The years have passed too quickly."

When asked about the reason for the success of their marriage, Bob said, "We both came from divorced families. I think we made extra efforts to make sure we stayed together. Of course, loving each other lots made it a whole lot easier to stay married." Karlene added,

"We were also involved in church so we had activities with other Christian couples."

They have this advice for couples considering marriage today. "Move to another town, far from your families for the first few years. Don't expect to have everything that has taken your folks years to acquire. Remember that your spouse is the priority in your life. Tell each other every day that you love them," said Karlene.

Bob said, "Stay faithful to each other, stay as debt free as possible, work hard at staying in love." Their faith is a very important factor to both Bob and Karlene. They agree that putting God in their home and their life was of major importance to both of them.

Her Sparkling Jewels

HER SPARKLING JEWELS

Made by Edie McGinnis, Rosemary Garten, Judy Lovell, Clara Diaz, Karlene Cooper and Judy Hill. Quilted by Nedra Forbes, Liberty, Missouri.

HER SPARKLING JEWELS

74" x 87"

Fabric needed:

- Light green – 3 yards (includes 2nd border)
- Medium green – 1 3/4 yards
- Dark green – 4 yards (includes outside border and binding)
- Rust – 1 yard
- Gold – 2 1/2 yards (includes 2" finished framing border)

You will need to make 30 blocks. Follow the paper piecing instructions on page 89.

Unit A

- Fabric A – light green – will always go in position no. 1
- Fabric B – medium green – will always go in position no. 3
- Fabric C – dark green – will always go in position no. 5
- Fabric D – rust – will alternate with Fabric C in position no. 4
- Fabric E – gold – will always go in position no. 2

Unit B

- Fabric A – light green – will always go in position no. 1
- Fabric B – medium green – will always go in position no. 3
- Fabric C – dark green – will always go in position no. 5
- Fabric D – rust – will alternate with Fabric C in position no. 4
- Fabric E – gold – will always go in position no. 2

For each block, sew the fabric in place. You will need four Unit As and four Unit Bs. After you have sewn the fabric to each unit, sew Unit A to Unit B along the diagonal. The only thing you really have to be careful of is making sure half of the quadrants in the block have rust in position no. 4 and half have dark green in position no. 4. Refer to the photo if you get confused.

After you have made the 30 blocks, sew them into rows. You need to make six rows containing five blocks. Sew the six rows together.

To make the borders, measure the quilt through the center. Measure vertically and horizontally. Write those numbers down.

Cut enough 2 1/2" strips from the gold fabric to make a framing border. You need to use your measurements that you just wrote down to determine the length of the strips. Decide how you want to sew your borders on. I sewed the top and bottom first, then added the side borders. When you do that, be sure to include the top and bottom border measurements onto your vertical strips.

For the second border, cut 3 1/2" strips of the light green fabric. Measure the length and width of the quilt again to get the measurements of the border strips. Sew the border to the quilt. I used a Wave Edge Ruler by Lily Marie to curve the edges. The ruler has two different waves and I used the widest one. Line up the ruler with the outer edge of the border, then use a rotary cutter to trim the edge. On the corners, line up a coffee cup saucer and cut around it. After trimming the wavy edge, press a seam line under. Sew enough dark green strips together for the last border. Pin the dark green border to the wavy edge making sure you have enough dark green to cover the uphill spaces as well as the downhill ones on the waves. Appliqué the wavy edge to the dark green border using your favorite method of appliqué.

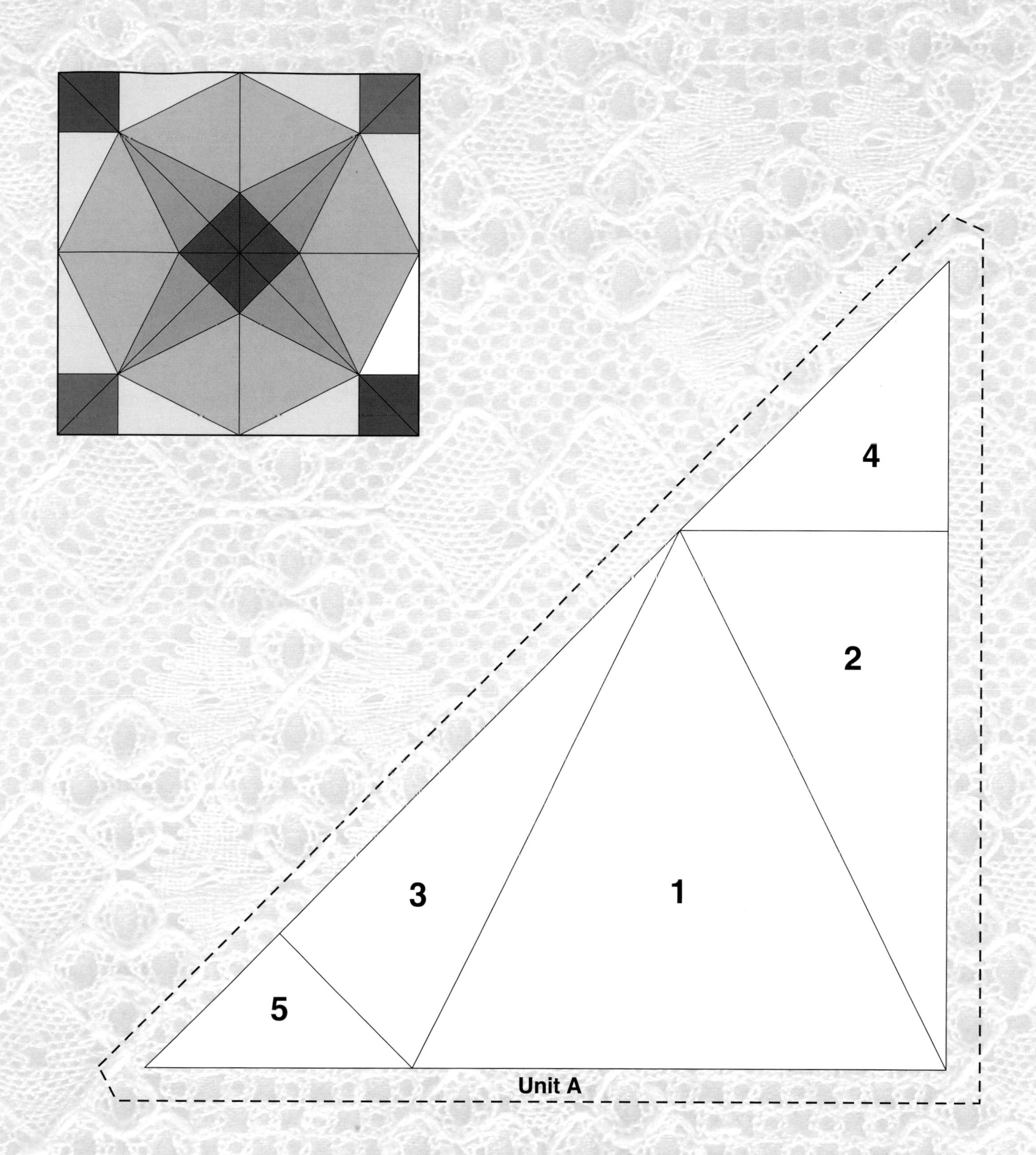
4
2
3
1
5
Unit A

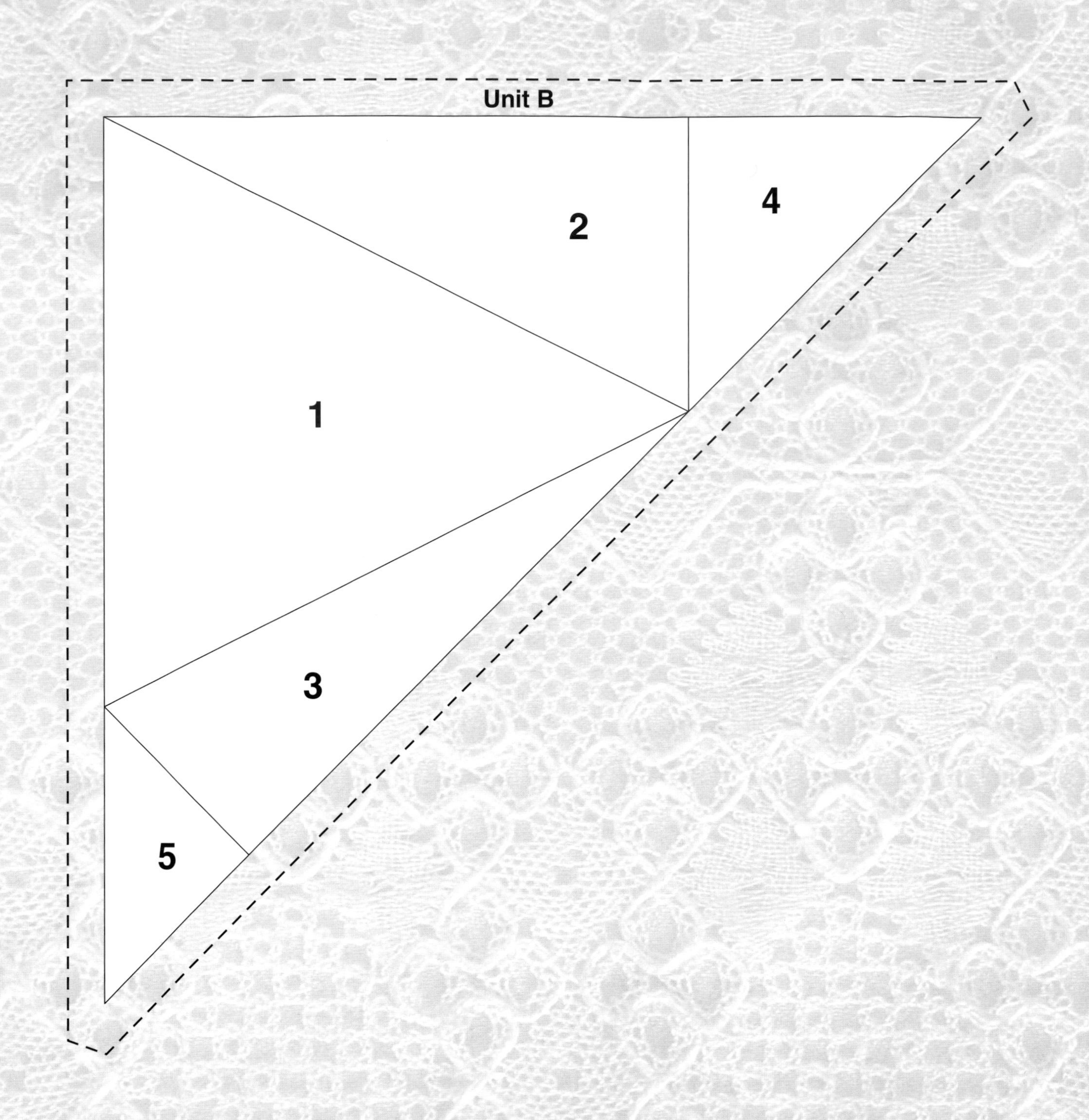
Unit B
2
4
1
3
5

The Jewel Quilt

THE JEWEL QUILT
Made by Carol Christopher, Blue Springs, Missouri.

THE JEWEL QUILT

Approximately 46" x 58"

Fabric needed

- 2 1/3 yards light blue
- 2 1/2 yards medium blue
- 3 yards dark blue

Follow the paper piecing instructions on page 89 and make 12 blocks.

To make each block, you will need to make four Unit A's and four Unit B's. Follow the position chart closely as the colors in the center 4-patch and the outside corners vary.

Unit A:

- Fabric A – light blue – will always be in position No. 2 and will be in position No. 5 in half of the units
- Fabric B – medium blue – will always be in position No. 1 and in positions No. 3 and 5 in half of the units
- Fabric C – dark blue – will always be in position No. 4 and in position No. 3 in half of the units

Unit B:

- Fabric A – light blue – will always be in position No. 2 and will be in position No. 5 in half of the units
- Fabric B – medium blue – will always be in position No. 1 and in positions No. 3 and 5 in half of the units
- Fabric C – dark blue – will always be in position No. 4 and in position No. 3 in half of the units

For each block, sew the fabric in place. You will need 4 Unit A's and 4 Unit B's per block. After you have sewn the fabric in place in each unit, sew Unit A to Unit B along the diagonal edge. Make sure half of the quadrants in the block have dark blue in the outer corners and half have medium blue in the outer corners. Refer to the photo if you get confused.

After you have made the blocks, sew them together into rows. Make four rows containing three blocks each. Sew the rows together.

Measure the quilt through the center and cut two 2" strips across the width of the medium blue fabric. Sew a strip to the top and a strip to the bottom of the quilt. Again, measure through the center of the quilt. You will need to cut three more 2" strips across the width of the fabric. Cut one strip in half. Piece 1 1/2 of the strips together, then trim each strip to equal the measurement through the center of the quilt. Add the strips to the sides of the quilt.

Using the above method, cut enough 4" strips of the dark blue for the outer border. Always measure through the center of the quilt.

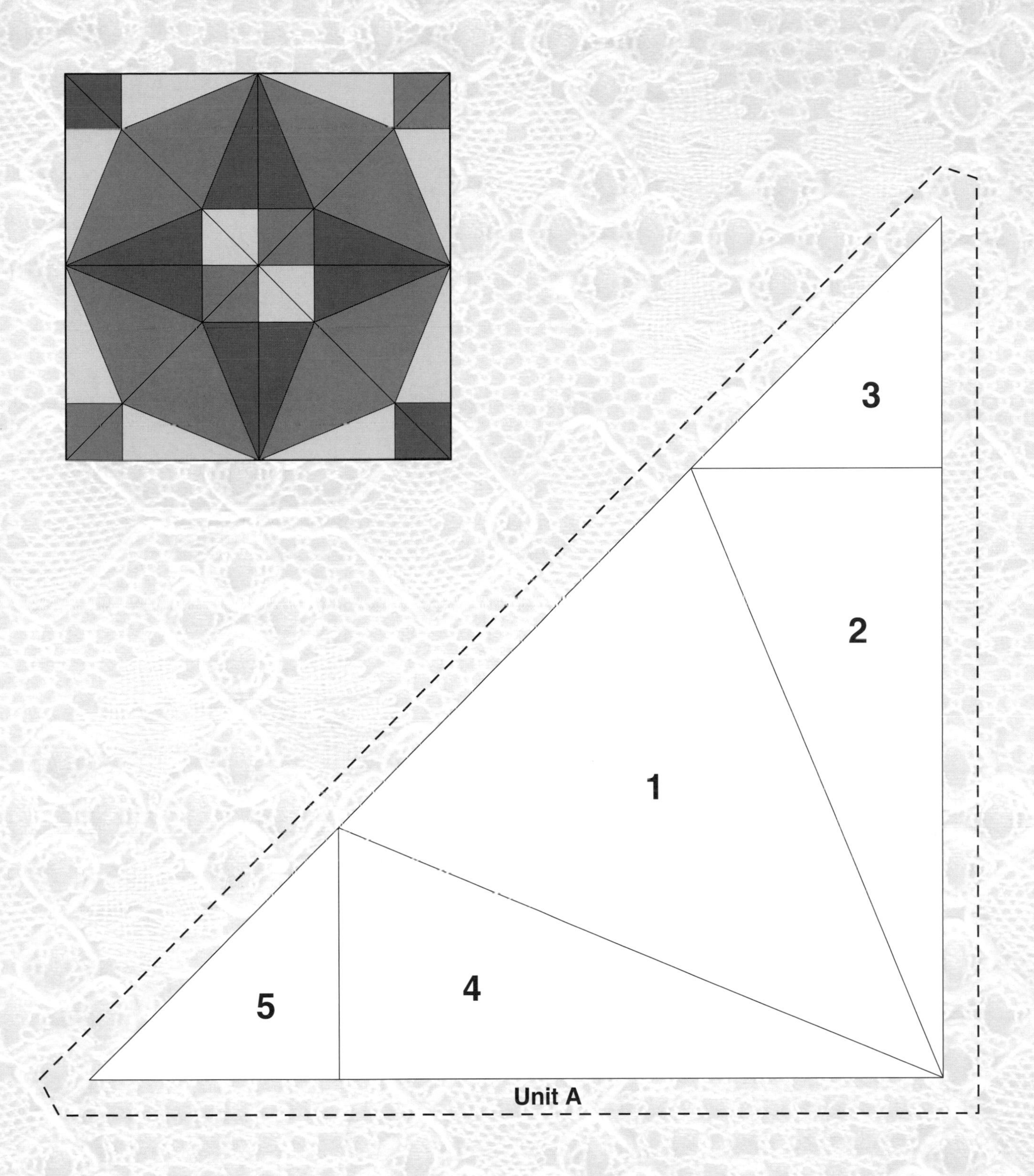
3
2
1
4
5
Unit A

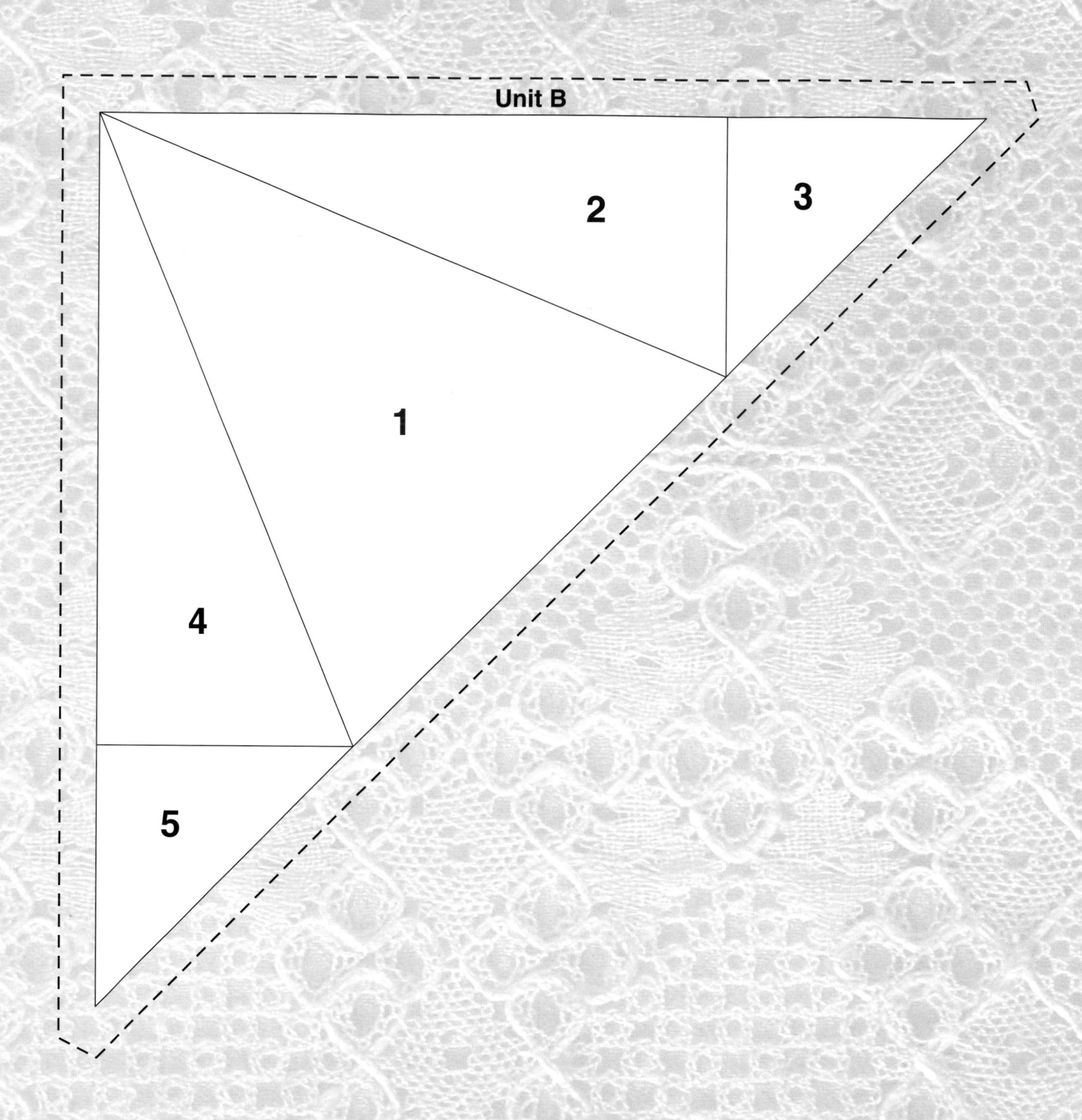
Unit B
2
3
1
4
5

BARB AND JOE DAY

Barb and Joe Day met in high school. Joe's family had moved to Excelsior Springs, Missouri, in the middle of his junior year. Barb was just a sophomore. They knew each other, but didn't date during their high school years.

After high school, Barb went on to college, Joe joined the navy. When he came home on leave in December of 1962, he asked her out. Joe picked Barb up in his pickup truck and took her ice skating on a frozen lake with church friends. He said, "We were sitting in her parent's dining room on New Years Eve when I asked her if she would marry me when I got of the Navy. She said, 'Yes,' and we were married July 13, 1963." They were blessed with one daughter.

Barb says she "just knew" that Joe was the right person for her. "I guess you could call it 'dumb luck' to end up with someone who treats me like I am the most important person in the world."

Joe said, "We have always been able to talk to each other and see each others point of view. She was the type of girl that I had always thought was right for me. However, she always tells everyone that I'm still on approval."

Their wedding was a formal event held at the Walnut Park RLDS Church in Independence, Missouri, with Joe wearing a tux for the first time in his life. He felt as though he was just a bit out of his element and thought it was the grandest affair ever. "I have since figured out that our wedding was rather moderate and that most grooms wear a tux."

Barbara thinks there are several factors that have contributed to the longevity of their marriage. "When we were first married, we lived in Newport, Rhode Island, far from family and friends. We were partners. We learned to depend on each other." Joe added, "We have always placed each other above everything else. Not a day goes by that we don't try to make each other feel like the most important person in our lives."

On July 13, 2005, they celebrated their 42nd wedding anniversary. For couples getting married, they offer these words. "If you don't mean it, don't do it. It means forever, not until something better comes along," said Joe. Barb added, "Make a commitment to be together. Cherish and care for each other."

Sparkling jewels, pearls of wisdom sparkling jewels,
pearls of wisdom sparkling jewels, pearls of wisdom
sparkling jewels, pearls of wisdom sparkling jewels,
pearls of wisdom sparkling jewels, pearls of wisdom

f wisdom sparkling jewels,
ng jewels, pearls of wisdom
f wisdom sparkling jewels,
ng jewels, pearls of wisdom
f wisdom sparkling jewels,
ng jewels, pearls of wisdom
f wisdom sparkling jewels,
ng jewels, pearls of wisdom
f wisdom sparkling jewels,
ng jewels, pearls of wisdom
sparkling jewels, pearls of wisdom sparkling jewels,
pearls of wisdom sparkling jewels, pearls of wisdom
sparkling jewels, pearls of wisdom sparkling jewels,

DIAMOND CIRCLE

DIAMOND CIRCLE
Made by Margaret Falen, Grain Valley, Missouri.
Quilted by Nedra Forbes, Liberty, Missouri.

DIAMOND CIRCLE

Approximately 90" x 103"

Fabric needed:

- 5 1/2 yards of dark red (includes yardage for borders and binding)
- 2 yards of dark pink
- 2 yards of light pink
- 2 yards of yellow
- 2 yards of cream
- batting and backing

To make this quilt, you will need to make 56 blocks. Follow the paper piecing instructions on page 89.

Fabric A – yellow
Fabric B – cream
Fabric C – red
Fabric D – dark pink
Fabric E – light pink

Unit A:

- Fabric A – yellow – position No. 1
- Fabric C – red – position No. 2
- Fabric E – light pink – position No. 3

Unit B:

- Fabric B – cream – position No. 1
- Fabric C – red – position No. 2
- Fabric D – dark pink – position No. 3

You will need to make four of each unit to make one block. After sewing all the fabric onto the back of the paper, sew Unit A to Unit B along the diagonal to make one quadrant of the block. Sew the four quadrants together to finish one block. See the photo or the block diagram if you get confused.

After you have finished paper piecing all the blocks, sew them together in rows. You will need eight rows and each row should have seven blocks. Remove the paper and add the 3 1/2" framing border. Be sure you measure your quilt through the center to determine the length and width of the borders.

Layer the batting and the backing and quilt.

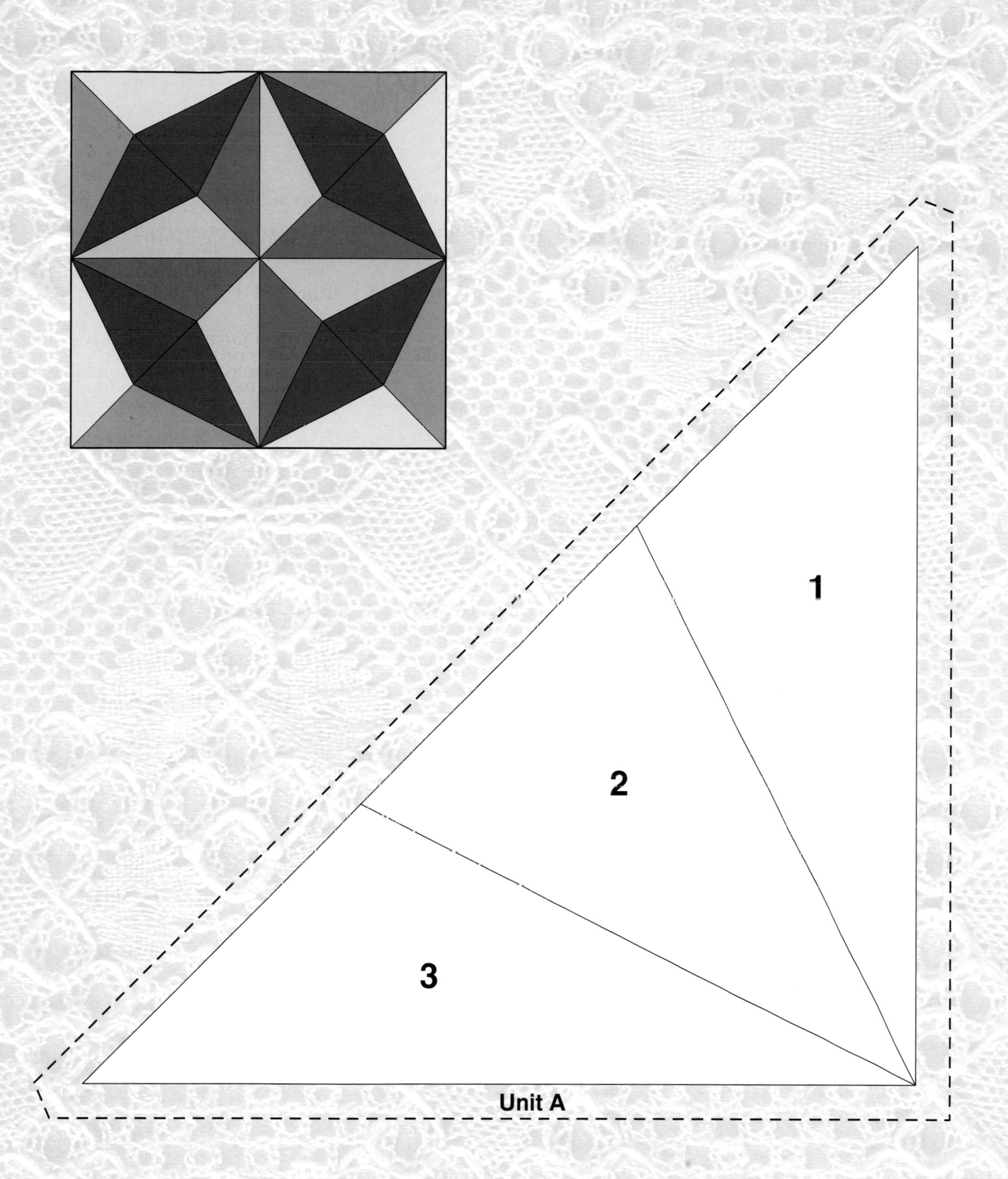
1
2
3
Unit A

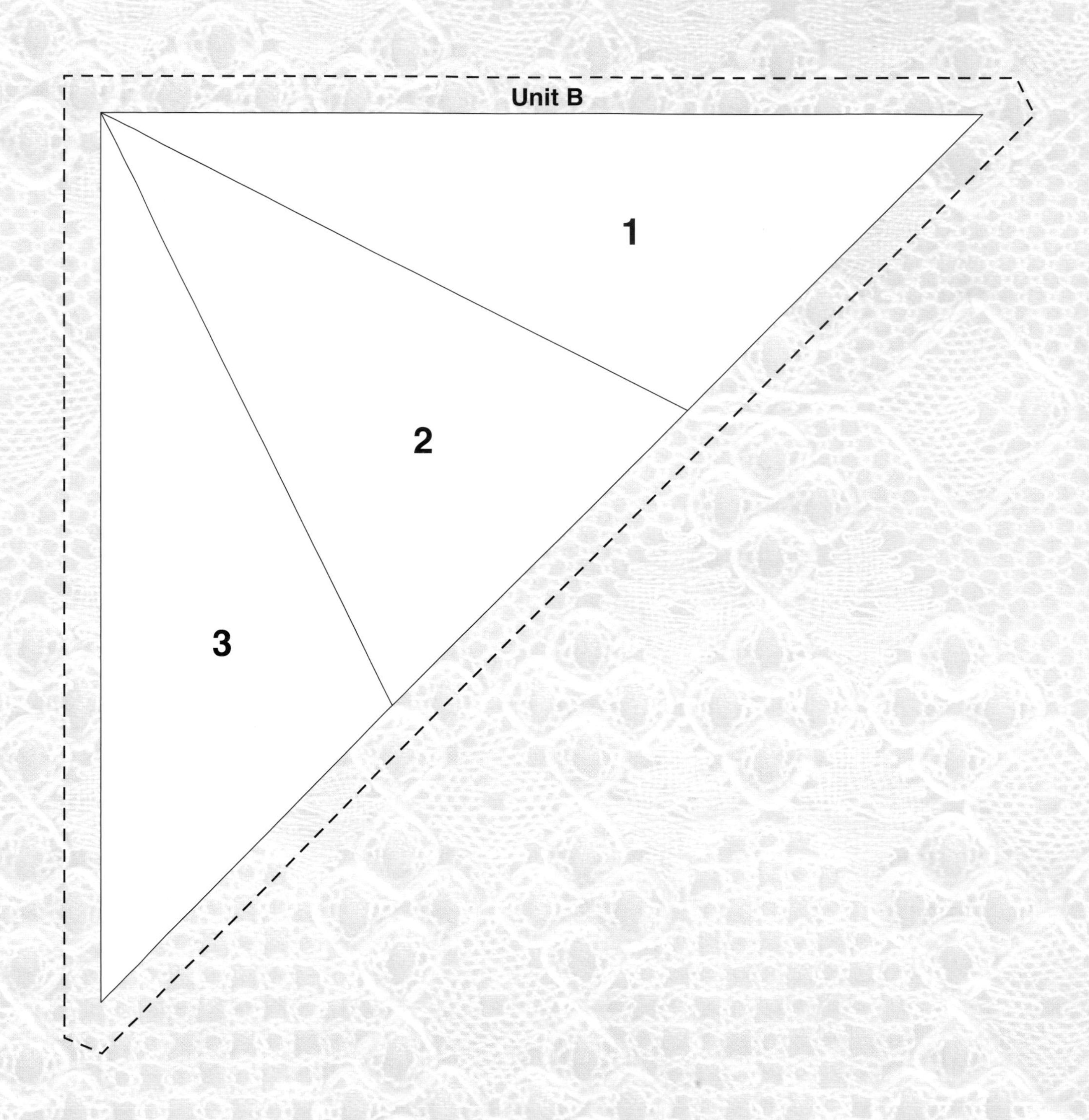
Unit B
1
2
3

RICHARD AND BETTY CONNELL

Richard and Betty Connell have a marriage that many would envy. After 52 years, Richard still looks at Betty as though she is the only person he can see.

Howard Cook, Betty's father, introduced Richard to his daughter. Richard had just gotten out of the army after serving in the Korean War. They say it was love at first sight. He says she was everything he wanted and thought he would never find. She thought he was handsome, a lot of fun and had good morals. Of course, it didn't hurt that he liked her either.

Their first date was a trip to Baker's Drugstore at 27th and Quindaro in Kansas City, Kansas, for ice cream. That date marked the first time Betty had ever been across the Kansas/ Missouri state line.

Six months after meeting, Betty and Richard were married. They had a large formal wedding at the Liberty Christian Church in Liberty, Missouri. Betty had two bridesmaids. They carried umbrellas filled with yellow daisies. Betty chose yellow roses and lavender gladiolas for her flowers.

When asked if they would do it all over again given the opportunity, Betty replied, "In a heartbeat. Richard gave me a life only few dream of. We have traveled the world and made many friends."

They believe the reason they are still together is due to their faith in God and the way they were reared. "We didn't go into this with the idea we could get out of it. We didn't think that the grass was greener on the other side of the fence, either," says Betty.

Their advice for couples getting married today is, "Always try to be good to each other and always, and I mean always, speak only good of one another to other people, and start the day with prayer together."

Sparkling jewels, pearls of wisdom sparkling jewels,
pearls of wisdom sparkling jewels, pearls of wisdom
sparkling jewels, pearls of wisdom sparkling jewels,
pearls of wisdom sparkling jewels, pearls of wisdom

sdom sparkling jewels,
ewels, pearls of wisdom
sdom sparkling jewels,
ewels, pearls of wisdom
sdom sparkling jewels,
ewels, pearls of wisdom
sdom sparkling jewels,
ewels, pearls of wisdom
sdom sparkling jewels,
ewels, pearls of wisdom
sparkling jewels, pearls of wisdom sparkling jewels,
pearls of wisdom sparkling jewels, pearls of wisdom
sparkling jewels, pearls of wisdom sparkling jewels,

Projects

PILLOWCASES
Made by Edie McGinnis, Kansas City, Missouri.

PILLOWCASES

Make a pretty pair of pillowcases using any fabric used in the quilt you are making.

Fabrics needed:

- 1 1/2 yards of fabric for the largest portion of the pillow cases
- 18" of a contrasting fabric
- 2 - 1/2" strips cut across the width of a third color of fabric

Cut two 3/4 yard lengths across the width of the fabric. You should now have two equal pieces.

Fold each of the 1/2" strips in half lengthwise and press

Pin the 1/2" strips to the long edge of the 3/4 yard pieces, right sides facing.

Cut the 18" piece of fabric into two 9" lengths. Fold each length in half lengthwise and press. Pin each folded strip to the edge of the 3/4 yard pieces with the right sides facing. Sew the three pieces together across the width of the fabric.

Now sew the top and side seams closed to finish.

AMETHYST NEEDLEPUNCH PICTURE

Made by Karen Kriens, Lee's Summit, Missouri. Framed and matted by Rita Briner, Quilter's Station, Lee's Summit, Missouri.

AMETHYST NEEDLEPUNCH PICTURE

Supply List

- 3-strand Igolochkoy Russian Punchneedle tool
- 9" square of Weaver's cloth
- 7" hoop with a secure lip
- Floss (Karen used Week's Dye Works floss)
- 2 Skeins of No. 1101 Light Khaki
- 1 Skein of No. 4121 Indian Summer
- 1 Skein of No. 3910 Mascara
- 3 Skeins of No. 1333 Lancaster Red
- 1 Skein of 1227 Bright Leaf

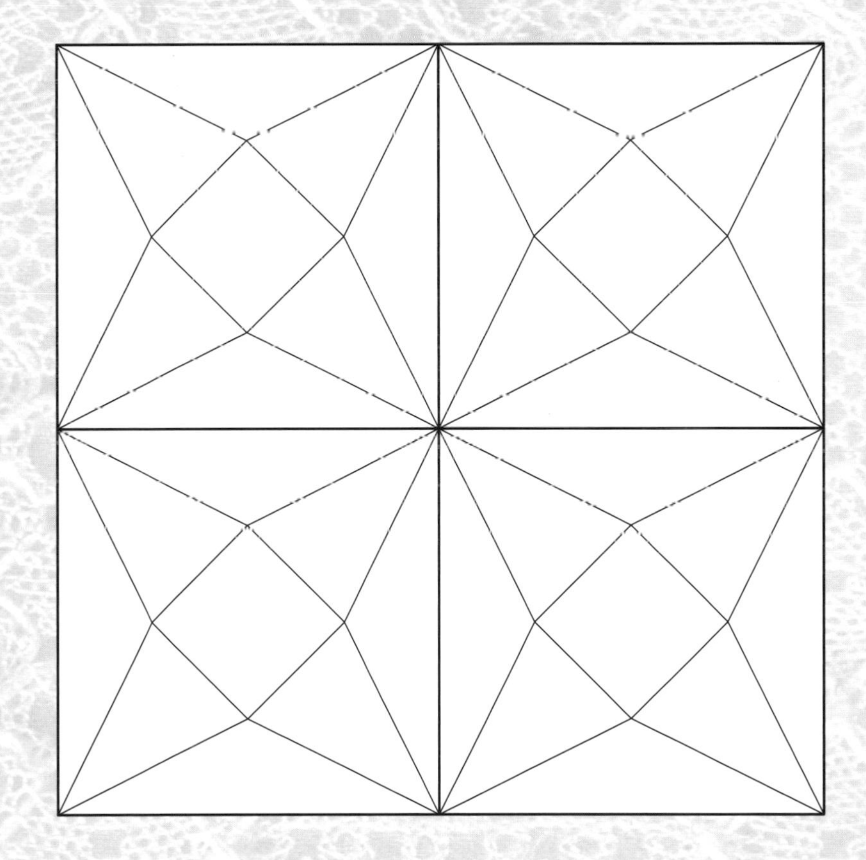

Use a light box and fine-tipped pen to trace the design onto the back of the Weaver's cloth. Be sure you have enough fabric around the design to fill the hoop. Follow the directions for doing the punchneedle stitches contained in the Igolochkoy Punchneedle tool kit.

Outline each area of the design, then fill in the larger portions of the shapes. Finish the background, then add 1 line of black and 2 lines of red around the whole design.

Mat and frame.

TABLE RUNNER
Made by Edie McGinnis, Kansas City, Missouri. Quilted by Rita Briner, Quilter's Station, Lee's Summit, Missouri.

TABLE RUNNER

Approximately 18" x 72"

Your yardage will be dependent upon which blocks you choose to make. Given that, I will give you yardage for the surrounding triangles and binding.

Dark Fabric – 1 1/2 yards

Choose any three blocks from the sampler quilt. I made two Jewels in a Frame and one Star of Diamond Points.

Cut:

- 1 – 18 1/4" square from the dark fabric. Cut the square on the diagonal, from corner to corner, twice to make the setting triangles.

- 1 – 12 7/8" square from the dark fabric. Cut the square on the diagonal, from corner to corner, once to make the end triangles.

- 2 – 9 3/8" squares. Cut the squares in half from corner to corner making four triangles.

Sew a setting triangle to opposite sides of the center block. Sew a setting triangle to one side of each of the two remaining blocks. Now sew the three blocks together on the diagonal.

Add one of the triangles you made from the 9 3/8" squares to each corner of the table runner.

Now add the two remaining triangles, sewing one to one end of the runner and one to the other end. You will want to sew the longest edge which is the bias edge to the runner. That will give you the straight of grain on the outer edges of the table runner.

Layer the top with batting and backing and quilt. Bind to finish.

BRIDE'S GARTER
Made by Stormy Lee van den Houten, Eugene, Oregon.

BRIDE'S GARTER

Supplies:

- 30" of lace
- 31" of 1 1/2" wide ribbon
- 15" of 3/8" wide elastic

Measure the bride's leg right above the knee. Fifteen inches is a fairly standard measurement for the elastic and generally works, but you would want to adjust the measurement now, if necessary.

Turn one end of the ribbon under 1/4" and sew it down making a small, narrow hem. Fold the ribbon in half along the length and carefully pin the edge of the lace between the edges. Overlap the hemmed edge of the ribbon over the raw end. Join the ends of the lace and ribbon into a circle and baste together.

Sew a seam along the very top (1/16") of the folded edge of the ribbon. This keeps the elastic from turning in the casing and gives a more finished look to the garter.

Sew the lace between the folded edges of the ribbon to form a casing for the elastic. Leave a 2" gap open in the seam so you can thread the elastic through the casing. Thread the elastic through the casing making sure it lies flat and is not twisted. Sew the ends of the elastic together, then stitch the 2" gap closed.

Add any embellishments at this time such as beads, ribbon roses, etc.

These instructions compliments of my sister, Stormy Lee van den Houten, of Eugene, Oregon. Incidentally, the lace you see on the garter is hand made bobbin lace.

TIME CAPSULE
Made by Edie McGinnis, Kansas City, Missouri.

TIME CAPSULE

Begin a family tradition by making your own personal time capsule. On significant occasions such as anniversaries, dig up the capsule, review the items in it and add and date any new items such as photos of you and your children. The time capsule can commemorate your lives together as a couple and a family.

To make the time capsule, purchase a watertight container such as a sturdy plastic container found in the housewares section in your favorite hardware or department store. Place items of significance to you and your spouse in the container. You might want to include items such as: a copy of a CD of your wedding photos, a copy of a CD of your favorite songs, a newspaper, complete with ads, from the day of your wedding, a flower from your bouquet, the groom's boutonnière, a list of the wedding party, a guest list, a letter telling how you met and a copy of the newspaper clipping announcing your engagement. Of course include any other items of your choice that have meaning to the two of you.

It is also good to add a journal. Each time you inspect your time capsule, write about significant events that have happened since you last opened it. Add it and new photos that are dated and have everyone in the photos identified.

Your personal time capsule will become a family treasure for years to come. You may even want each of your children to have one from the time of their birth.

OTHER STAR BOOKS

Star Quilts I: *One Piece at a Time* by *Kansas City Star Books* – 1999.
Star Quilts II: *More Kansas City Star Quilts* by Edie McGinnis – 2000.
Star Quilts III: *Outside the Box: Hexagon Patterns* from *The Kansas City Star* by Edie McGinnis – 2001.
Star Quilts IV: *Prairie Flower: A Year on the Plains* by Barbara Brackman – 2001.
Star Quilts V: *The Sister Blocks* by Edie McGinnis – 2001.
Star Quilts VI: *Kansas City Quiltmaker*s by Doug Worgul – 2001.
Star Quilts VII: *O'Glory: Americana Quilt Block*s from *The Kansas City Star* by Edie McGinnis – 2001.
Star Quilts VIII: *Hearts & Flowers: Hand Applique From Start to Finish* by Kathy Delany – 2002.
Star Quilts IX: *Roads & Curves Ahead* by Edie McGinnis – 2002.
Star Quilts X: *Celebration of American Life: Applique Patterns Honoring a Nation and Its People* by Barb Adams and Alma Allen – 2002.
Star Quilts XI: *Women of Grace & Charm: A Quilting Tribute to the Women Who Served in World War II* by Barb Adams and Alma Allen – 2003.
Star Quilts XII: *A Heartland Album: More Techniques in Hand Appliqu*e by Kathy Delany – 2003.
Star Quilts XIII: *Quilting a Poem: Designs Inspired by America's Poets* by Frances Kite and Debra Rowden – 2003.
Star Quilts XIV: *Carolyn's Paper-Pieced Garden: Patterns for Miniature and Full-Sized Quilts* by Carolyn Cullinan McCormack – 2003.
Star Quilts XV: *Murders On Elderberry Road*, a mystery book by Sally Goldenbaum – 2003.
Star Quilts XVI: *Friendships in Bloom: Round Robin Quilts* by Marjorie Nelson & Rebecca Nelson-Zerfas – 2003.
Star Quilts XVII: *Baskets of Treasures: Designs Inspired by Life Along the River* by Edie McGinnis – 2003.
Star Quilts XVIII: *Heart & Home: Unique American Women and the Houses that Inspire* by Kathy Schmitz – 2003.
Star Quilts XIX: *Women of Design: Quilts in the Newspaper* by Barbara Brackman – 2004.
Star Quilts XX: *The Basics: An Easy Guide to Beginning Quiltmaking* by Kathy Delaney – 2004.
Star Quilts XXI: *Four Block Quilts: Echoes of History, Pieced Boldly & Appliquéd Freely* by Terry Clothier Thompson – 2004.
Star Quilts XXII: *No Boundaries: Bringing Your Fabric Over The Edg*e by Edie McGinnis – 2004.
Star Quilts XXIII: *Horn of Plenty for a New Centur*y by Kathy Delaney – 2004.
Star Quilts XXIV: *Quilting the Garden* by Barb Adams and Alma Allen – 2004.
Star Quilts XXV: *A Murder of Taste: A Queen Bee Quilt Mystery* by Sally Goldenbaum – 2004.
Star Quilts XXVI: *Patterns of History: Moda Fabric Challenge* by Barbara Brackman – 2004.
Star Quilts XXVII: *Stars All Around Us: Quilts and Projects Inspired by a Beloved Symbo*l by Cherie Ralston – 2005.
Star Quilts XXVIII: *Quilters' Stories: Collecting History in the Heart of America* by Debra Rowden – 2005.
Star Quilts XXIX: *Libertyville* by Terry Clothier Thompson – 2005.
Star Quilts XXX: *Sparkling Jewels, Pearls of Wisdom* by Edie McGinnis – 2005.
Star Quilts XXXI: *Grapefruit Juice and Sugar* by Jenifer Dick – 2005.
Star Quilts XXXII: *Home Sweet Home* by Barb Adams and Alma Allen – 2005.
Star Quilts XXXIII: *Patterns of History: The Challenge Winners - 23 Quilt Designs Inspired by Our Past* by Kathy Delaney – 2005.

Project books
Santa's Parade of Nursery Rhymes by Jeanne Poore – 2000.
Fan Quilt Memories: A Selection of Fan Quilts from *The Kansas City Star* by Jeanne Poore – 2001.